Approaching
the Gospels
Together

BY THE AUTHOR

Jesus: Sketches for a Portrait

Approaching
the Gospels
Together

A Leaders' Guide for Group Gospels Study

MARY C. MORRISON

Foreword by Walter Wink

PENDLE HILL PUBLICATIONS

WALLINGFORD, PENNSYLVANIA

APPROACHING THE GOSPELS TOGETHER
A Leader's Guide for Group Gospels Study

Copyright© 1986 by Pendle Hill Publications
All Rights Reserved. No part of this book
may be reproduced in any form without
written permission from the publisher except in the case of brief quotations. For information address Pendle Hill Publications,
Wallingford, Pennsylvania 19086 .

Pendle Hill gratefully acknowledges the
private funding that has helped to make
this publication possible.

Cover Design/ Elsa Ph. Walberg
Book Design/ Carol Trasatto
Typesetting/ Fidelity Graphics, Holmes, PA
October 1986: 2,000
Printed in the United States of America
by Thomson-Shore, Inc.
Dexter, Michigan

The Greek on the cover is from John 1:1, "In the beginning was the Word."

Library of Congress Cataloging in Publication Data
will be found at the end of this book.

To all my Gospels Study Groups

Acknowledgments

These questions and procedures for Group Gospels Study did not come out of the blue. They owe their beginnings to Dr. Henry Burton Sharman's leader's guide of many years ago, *Studies In The Records of the Life of Jesus*, on which my dependence is strong throughout, and from which I have quoted a few questions directly. I have also found very helpful in a general way a set of unpublished questions formulated by Dr. Elizabeth Boyden Howes, for the loan of which I thank her.

Every group that I have ever led has contributed something to the growth of the material. In particular I want to thank Helen White, Phoebe Valentine, Dorothy Monteverde, Margaret Grosskurth, Peace Baxter, and Judy Bartels, who not only hounded me until I wrote it down, but also contributed many editorial and proofreading hours to help produce the book.

Order was produced out of textual chaos by the intelligent and resourceful keyboarding of Eve Beehler and the sharp editorial eye of Rebecca Mays. The layout owes its clarity and attractiveness to Carol Trasatto and the cover its effective design to Elsa Walberg. For this great help I thank them all.

MARY MORRISON
1986

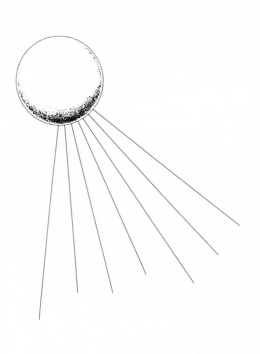

Contents

Foreword

The approach to Bible study outlined in this book is not simply an effective way of engaging people in the study of Scripture. Nor is it just a better style of teaching. For behind its deceptively simple appearance is a world of presuppositions and educational values that call in question the educational models that have dominated American and, indeed, all Western education for centuries.

The dominant educational model is based on the banking theory of knowledge. The student is relatively empty, and the goal of education is to fill the student as full of facts as possible. *What* the student is filled with is not all that important, as the current popularity of "Trivial Pursuit" illustrates. A successful education is considered accomplished when the student has successfully "mastered," that is, memorized and collated, a significant body of data. Little premium is put on the student's capacity to *think* with this material. It is enough if she or he is able simply to draw on the account on demand, a capacity which is demonstrable through tests and examinations.

Such a view of education is anti-democratic and autocratic, to put it mildly. The teachers and administration are the experts; they alone know what the student should know. In such a process the student is expected to have nothing to contribute. His or her task is largely passive, receptive, and uncritical. And while most of us have mercifully had teachers who transcended this model, it is, by and large, the decisive and pervasive style of current education.

The approach laid out by Mary Morrison in this book challenges every one of the banking theory's assumptions. She assumes that the student is already rich in experience, and can bring that experience to an encounter with the text that both clarifies the text's meaning and its relevance for our lives. The student's need is therefore not simply for data, though that is essential, but for insight as to the meaning of the data. The student is not a safety-deposit vault to be filled with precious facts, but is a living, choosing being already in the swim of life, looking for clues to the mystery of authentic living, restlessly seeking to unscramble the riddle of personal and social transformation. But this is also equally true of the teacher.

The very terms "student" and "teacher" are inadequate in this new model.

Both are seekers, both have insights to share, each can enrich the other. The "teacher" becomes an enabler, a facilitator, a person skilled in helping "educate" (from *educere*, to lead forth). This "leading forth" is done primarily through questioning, and it assumes a very high view of human capability: that the average person is able to think originally and creatively if challenged to thought by the germinal questions that originally brought the Biblical text itself to speech. That is, the group seeks, not "right" answers about what one "ought to believe," but attempts to divine the primordial and persistent life-questions which themselves inspired the texts being studied.

I have used this method for fifteen years and I have found no other approach for study, especially of the Bible, that comes close to this one in its power to evoke human transformation in the participants. I am pleased to recommend Mary Morrison's guide, for I am convinced that one of the deepest needs of our day is for precisely the kind of encounter with Scripture that this approach attempts to foster.

DR. WALTER WINK
PROFESSOR OF BIBLICAL INTERPRETATION
Auburn Theological Seminary
New York, New York

Publisher's Preface

Jesus told stories to people who wanted to hear. These stories lived in a community of people who had a long history and who recorded the best of their stories in a sacred text, hoping in that way to perpetuate their tradition. Jesus' own story in that text has been told and retold among those who still yearn to participate in a life-giving tradition. How do we empower the life of that tradition as we read the ancient text? In this study guide, Mary Morrison shares wisdom that provides the answer.

She and her Gospels Study Groups have been retelling the story of Jesus in their own words for over thirty years in a way that involves group members actively in the teaching. Their tool? A set of questions, forged in all those years of use.

Like the sacred story they seek to understand, the questions grew onto the page over time. When Pendle Hill opened more than fifty years ago, Henry Burton Sharman taught the Gospels by asking group members to share their own understanding of the text. On his departure, his student and trainee Dora Willson continued a similar course until her death in 1953. Her student and trainee Mary Morrison then taught the course from 1957 to 1977 with the same approach, modified by her own style. Since leaving Pendle Hill, Mary has continued to train leaders, enabling them to facilitate many varieties of denominational and non-sectarian groups.

This publication is a tribute to Mary's work. It is our pleasure to provide future leaders with such a proven approach whose strength is its rootedness in the Truth it serves. We offer it to all who yearn to teach and study the old, old story whose transforming power is as refreshingly available to us as it was to those who first wrote it down. May your courses, like Mary's, accomplish what a former dean of Pendle Hill, Parker Palmer, described so well: "create a space where obedience to truth is practised."

PENDLE HILL PUBLICATIONS COMMITTEE

THE APPROACH

Introduction

The Gospels are part of an ancient library, the collection which we call the Bible. This collection grew out of a tremendous idea, held by one small people in Asia Minor: that the Unnameable God, one, unique, the Creator of the world, had singled them out for special attention.

Their story of God's way with them is a long sequence sweeping through the centuries and making sense of all the things, good and bad, that had happened to the Hebrews in their vulnerable position within the ebb and flow of power and conquest in the ancient world. In the widest and deepest sense of the word, this story was their myth.

Myth is a hard word to deal with in our literal-minded era. We tend to think in contrasting terms of fact/truth and myth/falsehood. But the truth of a myth goes far beyond the question of whether or not it represents factual accuracy. Santa Claus is a myth with a very minimal historical basis. Abraham Lincoln and Martin Luther King are fully historical figures who have great mythical power in our time. The truth of a myth comes from its power to make sense of events, and to breathe a meaning into them that enables individuals or a people not only to endure their experience but to embrace it and grow continually in understanding it.

Paul Tillich once said, after a visit to Athens, that no one could stand on the Acropolis without gaining a sense of how the myth of Athena, goddess of Wisdom, had inspired, formed and developed the Greek mind and the Greek experience of life. Athena, a concept, a dream, a vision, not a historical figure, but what Jung calls an archetype, one of the guideline images within which and with which the human mind works.

Tillich added that the myth of Jesus Christ was the greatest myth of all. Jesus of Nazareth—a historical figure who lived and died within a certain period of time, surrounded by a certain culture, shaped by its limits, subject in all ways to the human condition. And yet also Jesus the Christ—a mysterious being so full of meaning that anyone who has really looked at him ends by asking Shakespeare's question:

> "What is your substance, whereof are you made,
> That millions of strange shadows on you tend?"
> *Sonnet #53*

That kind of compelling mystery is what gives myth its power. A myth draws us to it and makes us ask questions, eager to grasp the mystery so far as we are able. A myth does not make flat statements or spell things out; it is too rich for that. When we ask it questions, it answers; but the answers are not the same for everyone, or even for the same person at different times. A myth retains always a Delphic quality in that it speaks in answer to our questions, and our understanding of the answer depends, often drastically, on the set of mind with which we approach it.

To make things clear and sort them out is one of the strongest and most valuable human instincts. It has shaped the chaos of our experience into order, dependability and predictability. But a myth stands beyond all that, in the area of mystery, and asks of us the awe and respect that will keep it forever free to move within us, creating question, answer, and meaning.

Heinrich Zimmer in *The King and the Corpse*, his book on legends and myths, says: "They are the everlasting oracles of life. They have to be questioned and consulted anew, with every age, each age approaching them with its own variety of ignorance and understanding, its own set of problems and its own inevitable questions.... The replies already given, therefore, cannot be made to serve us. The powers have to be consulted again directly—again, again, and again. Our primary task is to learn, not so much what they are said to have said, as how to approach them, evoke fresh speech from them, and understand that speech."[1]

So it is with the Gospels and the great myth-symbol that they present to us: Jesus of Nazareth, Jesus the Christ. Our primary task is to learn, not so much what they are said to have said, as *how to approach them, evoke fresh speech from them, and understand that speech.*

How to approach the Gospels? Sometimes it seems as if there were no approach left open, "what they are said to have said" stands so impenetrably in the way. So many voices have said so much about them that our ears are deafened. So many eyes have looked at them that our eyes slide over the pages as if they were slippery.

They have become a lip-service part of our culture, deadened for us before they had any chance to be alive. The worst part of it is that we don't even know what happened. We only know that our feeling about them, if we are honest enough to admit it, is a blank, undifferentiated boredom. We can be persuaded to approach them as a duty; but we cannot even hear someone who tries to tell us that they are interesting. And if some brave soul tries to tell us that they are life-giving, then we hear the same old gospel-revival language that we are already immunized against, and we tune it out automatically. The Gospels are merely Holy Writ; how can they possibly bring us any good news?

What can they possibly say to us that they haven't already said when we were reluctant attenders at First Day school, or taking religion courses in college? We got the answers before we asked the questions; and now that we are asking the questions, the Gospels are almost the last place where we would think of turning for any answers.

What to do? How do we break down those invisible and seemingly impassable barriers?

Jesus generally dealt with the crowds who gathered round him by telling them stories. Not by laying down laws or answering questions or explaining things; just telling them stories.

So we might try approaching the Gospel first of all as if it were a story. We might try reading it as we read a novel, a really good novel, the kind we give our full attention to and expect to get a great deal out of; *War and Peace*, for instance; or *The Brothers Karamazov*; or Camus' *La Peste*; or Jane Austen's *Emma*.

What goes into reading a novel? We bring to it what Coleridge called "a willing suspension of disbelief." That is, we are not checking it out analytically against standards other than its own. We do not read it as fact if it is clearly fantasy, or prose-thinking if it is poetic, or tragedy if it is comedy. We give a novel the latitude it needs to say in its own chosen way what it wants to say to us. We enter its world, and let that world be slowly, gradually created round us, beginning with the first sentence of the first chapter. We interact with it.

Suppose, for instance, we open a novel and it begins, "Harry walked down the snowy street, looking in the shop windows." Immediately the questions begin. Who's Harry? Where is he? In a city? Maybe. Clearly not open country, anyway. When is all this? Winter? What century?

So we read on, carrying our questions with us. And perhaps the next paragraph mentions that the dresses in the shop windows have bustles on the back, and we begin to get an idea of the period. Perhaps the next page says that Harry is on his way to his law office; or that he is cold because his shoes have holes in their soles. We begin to learn a little about who he is; and we read on, asking more questions and finding more answers.

Now for the opening of Mark's account: "The beginning of the gospel of Jesus Christ, the Son of God." Here it is, Holy Writ, and immediately our minds go blank and all questions cease. We've heard it before, and we know the answers. But do we really? Suppose we read it as if for the first time, and as if it were a novel about Harry. Questions break out. Who's Jesus? Is "Christ" a title, or his last name? What on earth does it mean to call him Son of God, and in capitals at that? What's this word "gospel" that we never meet anywhere but here, and therefore (if we are reading as if for the first time) have never met before? Suddenly we realize that in that whole introductory sentence there is only one word that we understand, "beginning."

5

So OK, here we are at the beginning, and we realize that, as with any story, we have the whole sweep of what is to come in it to develop our curiosity and answer our questions, to let the theme grow and speak to us as it wants to.

Now begins the second stage of our process; to evoke fresh speech from this Gospels material. We already know the material too well, as we have seen. Even if we think we have never paid any attention to it, the words and themes are worn threadbare in our minds by centuries of everyday use in our culture.

The words have lost or changed their meaning. Take the word "minister," for instance. It was originally used to translate the Greek word *diakonos*, meaning servant. But now when we hear the word, we think of any authority figure whom others serve.

Or take "Gospel." Does it have a meaning? Isn't it just the name of those four books? We are surprised and think it a bit gimmicky when a new translation of them comes out on the supermarket shelf with a title that begins, "GOOD NEWS." And yet that is exactly what the word "gospel" means; it translates the Greek word *evangelion: eu*, good, + *angelion*, message; good message, good news.

Since this story was first written down, many of its key words have radically changed their meaning, not only through linguistic wear and tear, but also because the concepts that these words try to express are so foreign to ordinary, everyday human thought that tradition cannot pass them on. We each have to learn and continually re-learn them for ourselves through long experience of living with them, and living them.

Those concepts! And the words that try to express them! Faith. Sin. Forgiveness. Glory. Kingdom of God. Righteousness. Love, even love, the word we think we know best. When we try to grasp them, they slide away like watermelon seeds and leave us looking blankly around for what has disappeared. But perhaps we are in worse shape when we think that we have succeeded in defining them, for then we are casting in concrete what is meant to be a living experience, renewed daily.

Fortunately the well-spring of the Gospels is still here, still offering us the life and freshness of the original experience.

For those large-concept words there is help at hand in the many new brilliant translations of the texts that have come out during this century. Some, like the Revised Standard Version, the New English Bible, the Jerusalem Bible, The New American Bible, The New International Version, and the Good News Bible, are the work of committees and groups. Others are the work of individuals: James Moffatt, J.B. Phillips, Ronald Knox, Clarence Jordan. Any of these separately can bring the language to new life; and some or all of them, used together, can by their diversity set our minds to working. There are editions of the New Testament that set several traditions side by side: one put out by the magazine, *Christianity Today*, that includes four, another from Creation House that offers six, and a Tyndale eight-text edition.

Most of these new translations come in modern paragraphing and punctuation, complete with quotation marks to indicate direct speech and dialogue. No one not brought up on the old format can fully appreciate, for instance, how much more direct and personal the word of God is when it appears within quotation marks; a small change but very important.

The new texts do all they can for us; but fleshing out the dry bones of the concepts remains our job, and it is one that turns out to be a pleasure once we learn how to do it.

One way is to follow through on the discipline of reading as if for the first time, to the extent of pretending that each of the over-familiar words, faith, love, and so forth, is written in an unknown language. We have no idea what it means. We are foreigners intelligently trying to learn new words by the contexts in which they appear. It is a real exercise to take the word "faith," for instance, assuming no knowledge whatever of its meaning, and follow it through all its appearances in, say, the Gospel of Mark, gradually building up from the text itself a sense of the word's active and dynamic operation in the mind of Jesus. Or, better still, to do the same thing with all of the first three Gospels in one of the parallel-arrangement editions: Throckmorton's *Gospel Parallels* or H.B. Sharman's *Records of the Life of Jesus*, which set the texts of Matthew, Mark, and Luke side by side on each page for easy comparison, thus encouraging these closely-related but divergent Gospels to interact with one another in our minds.

A dictionary can be helpful too, particularly one that gives the history and origins of words and so opens up their overtones and undertones and all their possible meanings. A dictionary search can be especially rewarding if the word derives from Greek or Latin, because of their close relation to the earliest forms of our Gospels. And if the word-derivation dares to risk going still further back it can turn up such startling insights as that the word "truth" is related to the word "tree"—a comparison that calls up a host of images. In the dictionary, as in our search through different Gospels contexts in which a word appears, we are looking for its poetry, its living, active meaning.

The greatest help of all, however, is to assemble a group of interested people and look at the Gospels together, not as the merely literary "we" of the sentences above, but as the real "we" of a variety of individual minds thinking together. The different points of view represented even in a homogeneous group can be truly astounding. It is a real mind-stretcher to be one of a group engaged in frank and open looking-at and talking-about the Gospels. A dual process takes place. On the one hand, we come to see the great variety of insights which the texts contain; and on the other we come to a genuine respect for the many different points of view from which they can be legitimately and honestly seen.[2]

What we are working at, privately or in a group, is the business of turning what is for most of us dead and empty doctrine into living meaning that will grow in our hearts and give direction to our lives. We are encouraging the word/Word to speak to us.

All the great religious teachers say with one voice that to meet the living truth, we must let it come to us and speak to us *where we are*. We must be faithful to the text and to ourselves. Harold Goddard in his book on Shakespeare says: "The text must be as sacred to the reader as his facts are to the scientist. He must discard instantly anything it contradicts. But he must be as ready to strike life into it, from his own experience, as a scientist must be fertile in hypotheses."[3]

"As sacred... as facts." This should dispel any notion—if we ever had one—that our reading of the Gospels can be merely a springboard into the fantasy of what we would like to hear or what we want to be encouraged to think.

As we re-sensitize ourselves to read freshly, we must be prepared to collide with many events and sayings that we will not like at all. "This is terrible!" we will say. "It would be awful to have to think this! He can't really be saying that!" But he is; and our task at this point is to separate out what actually lies on the page from our reaction to it. First we must see as clearly as we can what is being said; then react to it.

The central character of this story is out to shock us, disturb us, upset us, just as he does the people in the story; and the question, with us as with them, is, how do we react to being disturbed? Will we be antagonized and refuse to listen? Or will we feel an inner stir of excitement, and open our minds?

If we come to the Gospels as we would approach a meeting with our most interesting, challenging, and sometimes exasperating friend, we'll be on the right path for a real meeting with their central character. If we bring our full, fresh attention in the kind of open response that we would have available for the person we most want to talk to or a letter of vital importance or a book we can't wait to read, then we will hold real conversation with the Gospels, and let them read us while we are reading them.

Then they will speak fresh speech to us.

And now, how do we understand that speech?

In reading a novel we find it easy and natural to adjust to the author's biases, background, and technique. We read *Emma*. Instantly we are in eighteenth-century England with all its prejudices and limitations (that we have outgrown) and its spaciousness (that we have lost). As we read we are not supposed to fret about the condition of the lower classes, the position of women, or the fact that none of the main characters seem to do an honest day's work; that kind of consciousness came later in history. We are supposed to let our thought move freely in a well-bred and gracious society, in which a wide range of human interaction is expressed not in passion, violence, or deep introspection, but in the nuance of a tiny turn of phrase. If we fail to make these mental adjustments we will miss the whole story.

The same process is required of us in all our reading. Even though Gibbon's *Decline and Fall of the Roman Empire* is history, not fiction, we still must move our minds back into the eighteenth century if we are to see accurately what the book is and is not saying.

But we lose sight of this requirement when we read the Bible. We have made almost a virtue of taking Holy Writ absolutely straight, as if its sentences were propositions in geometry, or more elementary still, 2+2=4. "It says *this*," we are told, "and *this* is what it means, no more, no less. It's a sin to juggle the word of God."

Now I too believe that it is the word of God. But to me the real sin lies in assuming that God always speaks in flat linear statements and never in poetry or fiction or riddles or jokes or dreams or anecdotes or folktales or drama.

The Hebrew Bible as a whole, that ancient library, needs a wide cataloguing system to include the tremendous variety of its contents: legend, lawbooks, history, biography, fiction, poetry. The Gospels, coming as they do out of that rich variety, hold it all in miniature. We will do them much less than justice if we assume that the same way of speaking, the same literary method, is always operating. We must read with a literary accuracy and integrity that will seek first of all the author's intention; and we must call up the mental acuity and agility to understand and work within that intention.

As readers of the Hebrew Bible we commit a second sin when we assume that God created those fine delicate responsive instruments, human beings, and went to all the trouble of developing the most responsive of them into the speakers-forth, the prophets, only to use them as simple dictating-machines. The fabric of prophecy is woven in a much more complicated way than that.

Similarly in reading the Gospels we are dealing with human beings, products of their own time and place, exhausting their range of thought and language to express the inexpressible as it speaks to them in their particular setting.

The author of Luke begins his account with a very valuable description of what sources he is using, whom he is addressing, and what he intends to do (Luke 1:1-4). He has been gathering up the written accounts; he has talked with some eyewitnesses; and he will put all this material into manageable order for the benefit of those (symbolized by the name "Theophilus = Lover of God") who have found their way to the Good News and would like to know more. Already we know one thing: we are to approach this story not from a distance but as if we were already inside it; it will not speak to us if we stand outside its circle arguing. We can sense too that this Gospel will be rich in varied material, and its point of view will be inclusive, rather than exclusive.

The introduction to Mark we have already seen; it is laconic, spare and uncompromising; and so (with a few garrulous exceptions) is Mark's Gospel, centering more on action than speech, and dealing with the mystery of what it means that "Son of man," a human being, is "Son of God."

Matthew's introduction is a genealogy of Jesus, beginning not with Adam, ancestor of all human beings, as Luke's genealogy does, but with Abraham, ancestor of the Hebrew people. It is the Gospel most rooted in Hebrew tradition and in Hebrew Bible prophetic "fulfillment"—a word to be taken not factually but poetically, as invoking many meanings and possibilities.

John we will look at later.

Whatever their individual variations (which are often great) in style, point of view, and context, the strongest impression that the first three give is of a central core of similarity out of which a central character speaks with consistency and power: Jesus of Nazareth, Jesus the Christ, Son of man, Son of God.

And this Jesus—what is his substance, whereof is he made? He is first of all a Jew, steeped in the Hebrew tradition, trained in its methods of thought and its codes of action, thinking deeply about the meaning of its history. Second, he is a genuine radical, one who turns back to the roots of his tradition in order to bring forth what grows continually green and fresh in it. Third, he is a challenger of all that is rigid and corrupt in his tradition.

These facts are so important that they can hardly be over-emphasized. They mean that if we are to understand his speech we must come with a Hebrew Bible in our hand, ready to look into the sources of his thought whenever we find (as we shall again and again) a reference that takes us back into his tradition. We must be ready to move within the deeply-ingrained Biblical habit of thinking and acting in symbols and speaking in paradox and parable. We must feel our way into the ingrained Hebrew sense of Covenant, the conviction of being a people chosen to understand and fulfill God's purpose. We must learn to accept as basic to the story the deep respect for Torah, the Law, that underlies the thought of both Jesus and his antagonists.

We must also have at least the bare bones of factual knowledge about the situation in which and to which Jesus was speaking. First-century Palestinian Judaism was a religion/nation guided by a dream. A small country, occupied by the Romans but dedicated to the service of God, it remembered its freedom and power under God's anointed King David, and looked for another Anointed One who would lead it into a renewed freedom and power.

In that small country, full of the comings and goings of all the peoples of the Roman Empire, pressed upon by all the temptations of those varied cultures, they lived, a people of God who had been told that through their wanderings they must keep themselves and their tradition pure and holy. "A stiff-necked people," God called them, stubborn and rigid and unable to listen to reason or compromise; but also full of determination and staying-power and undying endurance. No wonder God chose them. They held out against the pressures of time and place in the first century as they had throughout their history.

Many aspects of our twentieth-century experience stand in our way as we read all this. We are not a people of the Law, in fact we tend, with our own recent frontier history, to take the law into our own hands. We have no strong sense of being a people; we are more like a gathering of individuals. A phrase like "the Kingdom of God" has little spontaneous value for us children of the American revolution. We have theories of health and disease, we hold social and political values that are vastly different from those of Jesus' time. We know much more about history, science, politics and economics than first-century Palestinians; and much less about images and poetry and the art of finding meaning in our experience. Compared to the people who stood round Jesus and listened as he talked, we who read are college graduates in some ways and kindergartners in others.

When we have made the mental adjustments we need in order to read what is actually on the page, we can see that while Jesus lives fully within his time and space, he also transcends it and can speak to us across the distances and the years that stand between him and us. He is indeed, as he consistently called himself, "Son of man," *anthropos,* a human being. In that sense not exclusively a Jew, he can speak to the whole world. In that sense not exclusively a male, he can speak to the whole human race, transcending the male-female cultural and psychological structures as perhaps no one else ever has. In that sense not a first-century Palestinian, he can speak to all centuries and all countries. Because he is *anthropos,* a human being, he can speak to and for us all from the common depth that underlies all the cultural differences.

The wonder is that he could speak with an anthropos-voice at all in such a time of tension, defensiveness, resistance and sometimes open revolt. But he did, and does, and in so doing he brings us the assurance that the anthropos-voice can be spoken and heard in any time, however difficult—even our own, if we will stop to listen.

Jesus speaks with all the strengths and skills of his tradition: paradox; parable; the sense of the Torah; the sense of the truth; the sense of belonging to a coherent whole, both socially and intellectually; the authority of chosen-ness.

11

To take paradox first:

The famous saying at the heart of the Gospels, "Whoever seeks to save his life will lose it; and whoever loses it will save it and live" (Luke 17:33 New English Bible), is sometimes called the Great Paradox. It is a first-class illustration of what a paradox is; or, to make a definition by action, of what a paradox does. We read it; our minds are stretched two ways by the contradiction within it. No resolution is possible by any of the normal laws of logic and linear thinking; but the words carry a kind of teasing attraction, and our minds begin to work away at them like a dog gnawing a bone.

And that's a paradox! That's what it is and what it does.

Much of the great teaching of the world has been in paradox-form. The Buddha said, "I will show you sorrow and the ending of sorrow." Confucius said, "To reform the outer world, turn inward." Zen Buddhist teaching bases itself on this kind of brain-teaser, out of a firmly-held principle that all other ways of learning merely fill the teacup of the mind so full that nothing of value stands a chance of being added. The mind must be startled and teased into emptiness before it can let anything new burst in.

Paradox-teaching holds that out of this bafflement and consequent shattering of the old concepts, a total rearrangement takes place, something like what happens to the design in a kaleidoscope as it is turned. A fresh picture of the world, of oneself, of life, emerges—not out of the usual human either/or choice-tension, but in an instantaneous fusion of both/and.

The Great Paradox itself seems to demand of us a total rearrangement of our concept of life. If we let this mind-teaser have its way with us, life becomes not something that we own and take for granted, but a mystery constantly moving and calling us to follow where it leads—not looking back—carrying our cross (whatever that means), and trusting the mysterious process even into death and beyond.

A paradox is probably the most revolutionary form of thinking there is; it turns everything upside down. And it may also be the most conservative form of teaching there is, because if we let this disturbing upside-down process take place inside our heads, we are not likely to act violently in the world around us. We will have a new creative center from which to work, and our outward acts will grow, whole and beautiful, from the root of that inward newness. Confucius' paradox may be hinting at such a process.

Jesus used many paradoxes:

"The first shall be last, and the last, first."

"Blessed are you that weep now, for you shall laugh."

"Let the greatest among you become as the youngest, and the leader as one who serves."

"Whoever exalts himself will be humbled; and whoever humbles himself will be exalted."

12

Even what look at first like laws come out paradoxically too, in the "You have heard...but I say" sequences of the Sermon on the Mount, teasing us and asking us questions where we might have expected the old 2+2=4 approach.

Underlying these particular mind-blowers is a general paradox basic to Jesus' teaching: to be rich, happy, powerful, full of food and laughter—all our ideas of good fortune somehow get in our way and make us get in other people's way. "Whoever seeks to save his life..." about sums it up. No wonder it is called the Great Paradox.

Parable and paradox are related because they share the same indirect and challenging teaching method. We cannot take a parable linearly; we cannot reason it out. For modern readers, perhaps the best way of approaching one would be to ask, "If this were a joke, what would be its point?" And we would wait for that point to fly at us like an arrow and if we were lucky it would hit the target of where we are, and we would laugh.

Nobody really knows why we laugh. Books contain elaborate explanations. My own theory is that in laughing we respond to neatness and economy and speed of thought; we enjoy it as we do a good shot in a tennis match. It turns out right! And we exult in laughter.

As with a joke, if we truly "get" a parable, our first impulse is to laugh. Is— or should be. Impulses to laugh do not often stir in us when we read Holy Writ; we stifle them before they reach consciousness.

Fortunately, parables are part of nearly every religious tradition. Reading the unfamiliar ones may freshen our approach. Three good collections have been translated into English: *Tales of the Hasidim; 101 Zen Stories;* and *Tales of the Dervishes.* We are inwardly free to laugh as we read them; and they will teach us to begin laughing again at and with a fourth collection, our own, the stories Jesus told.

Parables, like jokes, not only amuse us; they also jolt us. They crack our closed minds open. As Sallie McFague says, "If the listener or reader 'learns' what the parable has to 'teach'...it is more like a shock to the nervous system than it is like a piece of information to be stored in the head."[4] Parables put together two things that we never thought of relating. Or they place familiar things in a wholly new setting. Or they illuminate an unfamiliar thing by the light of a familiar one. They are out to shock us, and they do.

Nothing whatever can happen between us and the parable unless we respond to it with our whole nervous system; unless we enter into its story and let it move us from one place to another in our thinking; unless we let it blow our minds. Jesus says, "If you have ears, then hear." And he is right. Not even the anthropos-voice can shout loud enough to make us hear unless we are ready to listen.

So we are to let the parables move our minds into a new dimension of

thought, a light and even graceful seriousness that is for the mind what danc-
ing is for the body.

It is not easy, however, for either Jesus or the crowds to which he speaks to
move lightly among the matters of the Law; they are the people of the Torah,
whose trust is in the word of Moses. Many of the clashes between Jesus and
his critics center on this theme, for his thought about Law is deeper and more
complex than theirs. No one can say that he slavishly obeyed the Law; no one
can say, either, that he disregarded it. His relation to it is best summed up by a
passage not found in our New Testament but available in an early text of
Luke: "Seeing someone working on the sabbath, he said to him 'Man, if indeed you know what you are doing, you are blessed; but if you do not know,
you are cursed and a transgressor of the law.' "[5] "Know what you are doing!"
It is a frightening demand, but one that Jesus makes of us throughout the
Gospels.

Another area of total seriousness for Jesus is truth. His opponents hardly
share that concern; much study of the Law has made of them, according to
the accounts, a group of casuists. Jesus is grimmer and more uncompromising about this than anything else in all his teaching. The great sin against the
Holy Spirit, the spirit of truth, is to be a hypocrite—to twist reality to suit our
needs and wishes, to fool ourselves and others about anything. It is a sin
against the eye that sees, the mind that knows, a betrayal at the center of our
being. "Blind guides," Jesus calls the casuists, and he is right.

A sense of prophecy grows naturally out of a concern for truth and is
Jesus' third area of deep thought and vigorous speaking-forth. The prophets
were giants of Hebrew tradition, and Jesus has clearly read them often and
thoughtfully.

What is a prophet? A foreteller of the future, we tend to think. But prophecy
goes deeper than that. The Hebrew prophets were first of all acute observers
and forth-tellers of their own times. They spoke forth what they saw God seeing in a present situation, often predicting the immediate future that would
grow out of this closely-observed present. Because they could see so deeply
into their own time, they described a basic and recurrent human pattern that
future readers could see as applying to their own time as well. Jesus was a
prophet in this same tradition, reading the signs of his times for all time.

Here he had help from his culture that we do not have. In our language
past, present, and future are distinct; in Hebrew thought they blend and coa-
lesce with a poetic freedom that is hard for us to grasp. Some linguistic scholars claim that the concepts a culture holds are conditioned by the way its
language is put together. Hebrew has two verb-tenses, one indicating uncom-
pleted, the other completed, action. This structure makes possible a free-
wheeling time-sense in which past can be present, and present can be future,
with hardly a break in the thought. In contrast, our language and the Greek in

14

which the Gospels first came to us have strongly time-bound verbs.

When we are trying to grasp Jesus' thought, we would sometimes do well to leave out the concept of time entirely and look for the timeless pattern that underlies the verb-tenses of our texts. For instance, it can be a rewarding exercise to translate the time-structured "Blessed are you that hunger now, for you shall be satisfied" (Luke 6:21 Revised Standard Version) into the Yin-Yang timelessness of "Being hungry is the other half of being filled."

Another feature of Hebrew language and thought is the ease with which a noun can refer, almost in the same sentence, to an individual and to a nation. "Israel" can mean "our father Jacob" one minute, and the next, the whole nation descended from Jacob. In Isaiah the "servant of Jahweh" moves, with an ease that bewilders us, from being an individual to being a whole nation, and back again. We in our time have a strong sense of separateness, even of conflict between the individual and the group; but for Jesus there was no such dividing-line. He moved within this coalescence of individual/group like its own child, as he was; and out of it he came to call himself Son of man—the individual who is one of, fully part of, and represents, the human race.

Kingdom of God is Jesus' fourth theme. It includes and sums up all the rest. It is made up of paradoxes and expressed in parables. It includes the Law and the prophets. It is both individual and social. It is past, present and future all in one. It fully embodies the triad of concepts that guided him: chosenness, servanthood, and relationship to God.

In developing the fullness of the Kingdom's meaning for him, Jesus uses all the tools of thought that he possesses: uses them, exhausts them, goes beyond them, to express the inexpressible.

And we as we read will be close to the heart of these Gospels in turn if we use and exhaust all our tools and mental resources to evoke from what he says about the Kingdom the fresh speech that will illuminate and fill with meaning our own times and thoughts and lives. For just as Jesus wanted the people of first-century Palestine to live in and be the Kingdom of their time, so he wants us to live in and be the Kingdom of our time.

FOOTNOTES

[1] Ed. Joseph Campbell, Bollingen Series XI, (Princeton: Princeton University Press), 1975, p.4.

[2] For information on how to start such a group and what to do in it, see page 17 of this book.

[3] *The Meaning of Shakespeare*, (Chicago: University of Chicago Press), 1951, p.12.

[4] *Speaking in Parables* (Philadelphia: Fortress Press, 1975), p.122.

[5] *Gospel Parallels,* ed. Burton H. Throckmorton (New York: Thomas Nelson, Inc., 1949), p.51.

Forming a Gospels Study Group

The procedures for starting a Gospels study group are briefly described in the material that follows. For a fuller discussion of these points, see the Procedures section at the end of the book beginning on page 147, and using the same headings. Two additional features are a list of helpful background books, beginning on page 159; and a glossary of words and phrases on page 22.

The first essential in starting a Gospels study group and keeping it going is a person who is eager and seriously interested. If you are that person, here is what you do:

Membership. Hold firmly to the concept that this is a *group* activity, in which the important elements are not the learning and expertise of one specialist or even a general level of prior knowledge, but the ease and openness with which the individuals within the group interact, and approach the Gospel material. With this in mind, begin to inquire around for people who might be interested in taking a fresh look at the subject. Groups can vary in size comfortably from six to sixteen, a size large enough for variety of insights, small enough for freedom of expression.

Leadership. It is tremendously helpful to have a leader skilled in group Gospels study. However, your group can proceed adequately with one learner/leader; or with a pair who work up the material together and alternate leadership; or with rotating leadership. The important thing for a leader is not to have answers, but to know how to ask questions; how to keep the discussion focused on the text and moving along at a steady pace; how to encourage all possible points of view; how to keep the more vocal members from dominating the group.

Schedule. A weekly meeting is desirable, if possible. It is a good idea to set meetings up in short units at first, ideally not more than four weeks, or at the most ten. Regular year-long study will develop naturally if the group goes well.

Group procedure. Group members should feel a responsibility to listen to one another, to express themselves as openly, freshly, briefly, and as much to the point as possible; and to encourage others to do the same. In their dealings with the text, they should maintain openness and encourage freshness by trying to read as if for the first time (this will put everyone, oldtimers and newcomers alike, on an equal footing) and by not bringing in any outside baggage such as doctrine, or even commentaries on the texts. There should be no coercion of any kind; the group is not trying to reach conclusions, but to open, vitalize and enlarge the thinking of each individual within it. A set of helpful rules for group procedure is printed on pages 156-157, and should be xeroxed and handed out to group members at the first session.

Questions. The Introduction has already presented some general idea of the kinds of questions that are profitable to ask of the texts. All questions on the following pages are cued in by number and letter to sections of *Records of the Life of Jesus* (referred to in the text as *Records*), a parallel arrangement of the first three Gospels made by Dr. Henry Burton Sharman. Originally published by Harper's, it is now being produced by the Creative Initiative Foundation, 222 High Street, Palo Alto, CA 94301.

A less detailed reference system is also given for *Gospel Parallels* (referred to in the text as *Parallels*), arranged by Burton H. Throckmorton and published by Thomas Nelson and Sons. This book is less convenient for group use than *Records,* but may be more readily available. If you use it with your group, you will need a copy of *Records* to use in your own class preparation. Both books are available through Pendle Hill Bookstore, Pendle Hill, Wallingford, PA 19086.

These questions have been tested and found effective in a teaching experience extending over thirty-six years. If you simply read through them they may seem a bit daunting. They are not meant to be read, but to be *used*, and in use they work very well. Some of the more closely text-centered questions may seem a bit picky, for example those on text relations; but they are essential as a background to the development of the general discussion. In practice you will find that the group can learn to work through them very quickly, five minutes or less to a section.

These questions and procedures are designed as a beginning step only, to help you in formulating your own questions and procedures as you work with the Gospels and the group.

And so, good luck, and much enjoyment!

The Opening Session

1. Get names and phone numbers. Have people introduce themselves very briefly around the circle (it's assumed that you are not sitting in rows, but around a table or in a circle around a room).

2. State the aim of this work, as you see it. The best general statement is: *To get a good look at the Gospels.*

3. Explain that this is not as easy as it sounds. There are real barriers in the way:

   - Overfamiliarity, which leads inevitably to a pervasive kind of boredom, though it will be hard to get people to admit this.

   - Respect for Holy Writ, which leads people to approach the material in an awed kind of way that keeps them from really looking at what it really says to them in this particular time and place.

   - A tendency to *study about*, rather than simply to study, which leads people to look at commentaries and theological interpretations, rather than the biblical text.

4. Explain ways to get over these barriers:

   - Accept the discipline of reading as if for the first time. Pretend you don't know anything about the central character or what happens to him. Refuse to think ahead in the story; stay with what you are reading now or have already read in the group.

   - Read simply and directly. As if, for instance, you were reading a good novel.

   - Use the text only—no commentaries or other guides. Trust your own reading of the text, as checked by the readings of other members of the group.

   - When you and the group begin to meet these big words—sin, forgiveness, faith, love, for example—loaded with centuries of theological content, free them up by insisting that their meaning must be

19

established each time from the saying or story in which they are used. A good way to accomplish this is to use the "missing word" technique, in which you all pretend that there's a hole in the manuscript at just that point where the big word comes, and ask, "What word or words would you put in here, guessing from the context?"

- Similarly when you meet stories or sayings that seem to bear on doctrinal concepts—the divinity of Christ, for example, or justification by faith, or election and grace—set them gently aside, and simply ask of the text, "What's the *most* that's being said here? What's the *least*?" This maximum/minimum approach can be a big help at times like these.

These five disciplines may seem silly to you at first, but you will soon see that the rewards are very great, for the meaning of the text will grow out of the text itself as you go along. In other words you are going to do all of your work right there with the text, and you are going to have all of your rewards right there too.

5. The discussion group method is a great additional help. This is the method by which this class will proceed. Lecturing will be at an absolute minimum—only enough to provide background or guidance as needed, and it should hardly be needed at all. The leader's function is simply to ask questions about the text, and to keep the group on the track and moving along well. (Here introduce the Group Members Sheet, pages 156-157, read together and discuss.)

6. Pass around Henry Sharman's *Records of the Life of Jesus*. Explain very briefly how it works, using the Introduction on pages v and vi of the book, which you will need to have read and understood yourself beforehand, in order to paraphrase it for the group. They will come to understand the book's workings best by simply using it; but a quick look at the column arrangements, the use of Roman and italic type, the footnotes, and such other points as you want, will be a good start. Section numbers precede each section and are also printed at the upper left and right corners of the pages. Capital letters within the sections are used to indicate different kinds of text relations, or separate units of thought. On page 15, for example, text relations are indicated as follows: A is only in Mark; B only in Luke; C in Matthew/Luke; D in all three; and so on. Page 16 illustrates the use of letters to indicate separate units of thought. This system is a tremendous facilitator for cross-referencing, of which you and the group will be doing a great deal as time goes on.

7. You will be asked what version of the Bible Sharman has used. It's the En-

glish Revised Version of 1882. It is a good text, even now, as being very close to the Greek of the New Testament. You hope, however, and expect that each class member will supplement it by following along in her or his own favorite version, being ready to read aloud from that as it contributes understanding to the Sharman text. Until the book is re-done in Revised Standard Version this is the most usable arrangement for group work and that is why you are using it.

8. Throughout the study you and the group will be following the angel's instruction to Mary in §4 B Luke, "You shall call his name Jesus." It is not disrespectful, as we vaguely feel; it is accurate, and helps us avoid confusion when later (very soon in fact) we shall be discussing the concept of the Christ. So "Jesus" it is—and hold them to it.

9. Explain that the group will begin work where Mark begins, at Section 17, where the adult Jesus comes to John for baptism. There are two reasons for this:

   - Invite the group to leaf through the first 16 sections, not reading, simply looking. Ask them how much parallelism exists among the three Gospels, reminding them how to get their cues from Roman type, italics and empty spaces. The answer should emerge that there is no direct parallelism, and almost no similarity of the material at all. It is good, also, to note that there is no Mark for this material, and to note that the parallelism of the three texts (leaf quickly through the book, looking particularly at §36-38, §80-114 and §148-151) breaks down completely when Mark is absent. So it is better for the group work to start where the three Gospels begin to march in step.

   - Most of the doctrinal matters that the churches have been hung up on for the last 2000 years occur in sections 1-16; it is easier not to get tangled up in them until the group has more experience with the text and is more cohesive.

10. Nevertheless, as a preliminary short exercise discussion of the preface to Luke will show the group how much information the text will yield if approached directly. Have the group read §1, Luke (the preface to Luke) carefully, asking *of the text* (no other books referred to) such questions as: What kinds of sources has the author used? How close was he to the events he is reporting? Who or what is his audience? From what point of view was he writing? What biases or prejudices, if any, does he show? What clues are there, if any, as to when roughly, this Gospel was written?

11. Groups have found these words and terms puzzling; here is how they are used:

Document Q   The hypothetical source document—Q, standing for the German word *Quelle*, or Source—used by Matthew and Luke in the places where they show close parallelism without Mark present to account for it.

Synoptic Gospels   The first three Gospels, so-called from the Greek *syn*, meaning together, and *opsis*, meaning sight—indicating that these Gospels give their accounts from the same general point of view.

text situation   It is assumed throughout this book that the relations among the three Synoptic texts are as follows: Mark is the direct source for much of the material in Matthew and Luke. Matthew and Luke have another large area of parallelism coming from a source which we do not have—the hypothetical Document Q. In addition Matthew and Luke each have material to be found only in them. John is assumed to have only indirect connections with the other three Gospels.

content   (accent on first syllable) as used in these questions, the main substance or meaning of what is said in the text.

context   the whole situation surrounding some single word, saying, or event.

koan   a Zen Buddhist word for a short, obscure and challenging statement, designed to block the logical mind and open it up to deeper thinking processes.

parable   a word with a wide range of meaning as used in the Gospels. Sometimes a proverb, more often a story, short or long, making a koan-like point about an incident or a situation, forcing the hearers to think more deeply into it, or think differently about it.

paradox   an apparently self-contradictory statement with the same koan-like purpose, and, like a parable, often embodying a truth which could not be expressed in any other way.

precept   a rule or direction for the guiding of one's life, attitude, or thought.

process   as used in this book this word picks up primarily the dictionary meaning, "a particular method of doing something," mostly as applied to the way in which Jesus lived his life, or the way in which he tried to instruct other people to live and act.

Now you are ready to begin getting a good look at the Gospels.

THE QUESTIONS

The First Three Gospels

SECTION 17 *Records* (1-4 *Parallels*)

Preparation for § 17: Review notes in point 9 in the Opening Session. Then, leaf through Sections 1-16, noting direct parallelism (none); absence of Mark; indirect parallels (in italics—very few); and then show how they all suddenly begin to be parallel in §17, e.g. Matthew/Luke dependent on Mark (§17 DEP); Matthew/Luke dependent on the hypothetical Document Q (§17 LMQ and final phrase of P); and Matthew and Luke each using material that they alone have, e.g. §17 N-O Luke.

1. Now for Section 17. Read as if for the first time—aloud, or silently together; you can ask which the group prefers. If aloud, usually the most effective way is to read Mark consecutively and ask the group to note the variations in Matthew and Luke as they go along. Do not stop to discuss, however, but move on.

2. Focus in on §17 A Mark by asking: If you were really reading this for the first time, how many unknown words or phrases are here? Gospel? Establish meaning from §17 R Luke and Sharman's footnote. Jesus Christ? Is this a first and last name or a name and title? Establish from §17 O Luke the fact that Christ is a title. Son of God? Note Sharman's footnote. The meaning of the phrase will begin to be established in §18 and §20.

3. What picture does §17 give of the general climate of the times into which this unknown central character, called simply "Jesus" (§18 A), comes?

4. What is the political situation described in §17 B Luke? Roman occupation and domination; the area divided into four (meaning of "tetrarch") parts; Jewish religion still allowed to function: a full description is all right there in the text, and the text is all the group needs in order to get on with the work. This is the place to begin resisting a temptation to look it all up in a commentary; it's a great chance to demonstrate that they can and should work *directly with the text.*

5. What is the religious situation? (Hebrew religion still functioning, §17 B; John the Baptist a prophet in tension with the religious establishment, C-N; expectations of the times, O-Q.)

6. What kind of prophet is John? Work on descriptions in C-J. What are the details of his message as reported in MN and described in C-H? Encourage the group to be clear about what the message *is* and what it *is not.* If the group has any Hebrew Bible knowledge to draw on, ask them if he is like Hosea, for example, or like Amos. (Where the group draws a blank, you as leader can gently supply a minimum of information. For example, here you can say that Amos tends to scold his readers, while Hosea speaks in

25

the image of a loving husband urging his wife to return to him.)

7. Baptism. Repentance. Kingdom of heaven at hand. What would these words mean to you if you came to them from the Hebrew heritage as John the Baptist's hearers did? (The only baptism that John the Baptist's hearers would be familiar with is a general cleansing and purifying, plus the ritual washing required of converts to Judaism. Someone will probably bring up the Essenes; but that too was repeated cleansing and purifying.)

8. What is John the Baptist's message in §17 N Luke? (To refer to him always as John the Baptist avoids confusion with the disciple John). Is he asking them to change their situation or lifestyle? What is he asking them to do?

9. What can we learn purely from the text, using nothing else, about the meaning of the phrase "the Christ" in §17 O Luke? (that it is a title; that the Christ is expected.) If desired, look back at §4C, §10 CD, §11 BC for other meanings. (political king; savior; God's chosen successor to David as King.)

10. How does John the Baptist see the "coming one?" What does he expect? See §17 PQ. How closely is this "coming one" associated with "the Christ?"

11. How closely is this "coming one" associated with Jesus by name?

SECTION 18 *Records*   *(6 Parallels)*

What are the differences among the texts? This question, which should precede your discussion of every section, is actually very simple and should take no more than a minute or two. The group simply notes, saving for discussion for later, where and how Matthew/Mark/Luke differ from one another. For instance, in this section, B is only in Matthew. ACD are in all three in Roman type, with small but significant differences in their wording which will be examined as the material is discussed.

Theme I: Jesus and his tradition

1. What does it tell us about Jesus that he came to John the Baptist for baptism?

2. What if anything does his coming to John the Baptist indicate as to his relation with his tradition? Uncritical; rebellious; or what else?

Theme II: Baptism experience of Jesus

1. Who *saw*, according to Matthew? Mark? Luke? See CD.

2. Who *heard*, according to Matthew? Mark? Luke?

3. How would you describe this experience for Jesus? Inner; outer; or what?

4. What do you make of the images surrounding the experience: clouds opening, dove, voice?

5. What is the content of this experience for Jesus?

6. Is this an experience similar to any experiences that we have? If so, what kind or kinds?

7. How do we choose or find out what we are to do in life? (vocation)

8. What are the possible temptations connected with this opening and accepting kind of experience?

9. (You may want to do this first.) Going back to B, the part of the story that is only in Matthew, what happens between John the Baptist and Jesus? What does John the Baptist see in Jesus? (A superior being; the Christ; the mighty "coming one" of §17 P; or what?) How does Jesus respond to this high evaluation?

10. If there is time, as a wind-up and to show that §18 and §20 are basically halves of one experience, move over into §20, *Mark only*, asking why ("Straightway") this experience follows immediately after the experience in §18. What is the nature of this desert experience? What do these various images contribute: wilderness; Satan; forty days; wild beasts; angels?

SECTION 20 *Records* (8 *Parallels*)
The Temptations

What are the text differences?

Theme I: The other half of the experience in §18

1. How closely is this connected with §18 according to Mark?

2. What is the nature of the experience outlined in Mark? Why is it

"the Spirit" that drives Jesus to the wilderness? What does "the Spirit" do in §18?

3. "Tempted of Satan"; "with wild beasts": How, if at all, do these connect with those in §18: the voice; heavens opening; dove?

4. How would you describe the total process outlined in Mark §18 and §20?

Theme II: The nature of the choices made by Jesus in §20 Matthew/Luke

1. "If you are the Son of God...": What is the tempter implying? What are all possible implications of the phrase "Son of God?"

2. Where does Jesus find his answers in BCD (using the Matthew order)? Where does the tempter find his quotation in C? What source are both Jesus and the tempter using?

3. What does it mean that the spirit "led" or "drove" him to confrontation with Satan? What do we learn here as to the processes of the Spirit? Is Satan an outer or an inner force? Is this whole experience an outer or an inner one?

4. What does Jesus turn down in B? Why?

5. What does Jesus turn down in C? Why?

6. What does Jesus turn down in D? Why?

Theme III: How to take this story

1. Repeat question 3 in Theme II above.

2. Do you think that Jesus is here dealing with something he already knew was wrong, or that he decided was wrong at the end of the period of testing? What is the essential difference between considering the possibility of doing something one knows is wrong, and trying to find out what the right really is?

3. In the Matthew/Luke accounts are we to take the temptations described in BC/ED as personal ones; messianic ones; both; neither; or what?

4. What is the basis for Jesus' refusal in all three cases? Where does he find his insight or his authority for his refusal?

5. What is the function of the devil in the episode?

6. What does this episode tell us, directly or indirectly about Jesus' relation to the messianic issue of his time: see "Whether haply he were The Christ" §17 O.

7. What does this episode tell us about what "Son of God" meant to Jesus?

8. What does it tell us about Jesus himself? What does it tell us about what his work will be?

9. What is the meaning of the word "tempt" in this section?

10. To what extent are the ideas that Jesus decided were wrong prevalent today? What forms do they take?

11. What light does this section throw on Jesus' attitude toward expecting God to work in supernatural ways? Toward expecting special treatment of any kind? Toward the use of power?

SECTION 21 *Records* (*9 Parallels*)

1. Significant differences among the texts?

2. A Matthew/Mark: "delivered up": meaning? Why not in Luke? (Cf. §17 R.)

3. What is the relation of Jesus and John the Baptist as indicated here? How dependent upon the message of John the Baptist is this earliest message of Jesus in C? How similar is it to that in §17 C?

4. What meaning would the message in §21 C have for Jesus' hearers? For instance what would "Kingdom of God" mean to them? Take time to note "Kingdom of heaven" in Matthew; and "Kingdom of God" in Mark; comment that this is so throughout the two Gospels. Are the two phrases synonymous? If so, why the difference in phrasing?

5. Look at C in all three Gospels. What had Jesus apparently decided to do, after saying no to all the tempter's ideas in the desert?

6. In B Matthew, what is the meaning of "fulfilled?" Fulfillment of what is spoken by the prophets—how, in what sense? What is the point of this Hebrew Bible passage as used here?

29

SECTION 22 *Records* (10 *Parallels*)

1. Point out that these accounts connect only at §22 CDH. Then focus on the Lukan account.

2. Give them these key questions to hold in their minds while reading: What is the difference between the reaction of the crowd in C, and that in K? What causes this change?

3. In the Isaiah quotation in B, to whom does the word "me" refer?

4. What does Jesus' use of this passage indicate about his idea of his own purpose and function? What kind of mission does this passage describe? What hopes does it raise?

5. What point is made by the two proverbs cited in GH? What hopes are dashed or disappointed?

6. What point is made by the two Hebrew Bible stories repeated in I?

7. Why are his hearers so angry?

8. What picture of Jesus do you get from this whole episode? From K in particular?

SECTIONS 23, 27 *Records* (11, 17 *Parallels*)

1. Text differences?

2. Point out that here are two different stories of the calling of the first disciples. Then focus on Matthew/Mark.

3. How were the men attracted to Jesus in Matthew/Mark?

4. "Fishers of men": What is the scope and meaning of this image? Why did Jesus choose fishermen to be his earliest followers? This is a pair of questions for the imagination to play with.

5. Now for the Lukan version. How were the men attracted to Jesus?

6. "Depart from me": Why is there this reaction on Peter's part?

7. Pick up the word "sinful" as one of the ones to pretend we don't know the meaning of. ("There's a hole in the manuscript here.") What is the content of the word "sinful" *in this context alone?*

8. How does Jesus deal with Peter's reaction?

9. How do you account for the catch of fishes? Give all possible explanations. These categories can be a basis for a consideration of later miracle-stories.

10. How does Peter as he appears in this story reveal himself to us and our lives? (This is the first example of a technique that many people find very revealing and helpful, i.e. to encourage the group to identify with the different kinds of people who gather round Jesus be they the sinners, the self-righteous, the disciples, the members of the crowd, the rich, the poor, the women, etc.)

SECTIONS 24-26, 28 *Records* Jesus' Healing Ministry   **(12-16, 45 *Parallels*)**

These sections include a series of healing stories, to be approached open-mindedly, trying to avoid on the one hand, "Well, of course he could do this because he is Jesus/Son of God and of course he can do anything" and on the other hand, "This is impossible; I don't believe a word of it."

1. What is happening in these stories? (In contrast to: What is the *tradition* about what is happening? Or what do *I* think is happening? Stick to the descriptions and try to act as if there were or you had no preconceptions.)

2. What is our current thinking about health and disease (e.g. germs, vitamin deficiency, mental illness)? Spell out as much as possible what we think causes and cures physical and mental illness.

3. What appears from these stories to be the first-century theory or theories of health and disease?

4. In each story, setting aside whether we believe or disbelieve, what is *described as happening*, both by first-century theories and by ours.

   a) In §24: What ails the man? What causes his illness? How is he healed? "Taught with authority" What is the meaning of what the man says to Jesus in §24 C?

   b) §25: What distinction is indicated here between physical and mental illness? What is the meaning of the devil's recognition in §25 EF Mark/Luke? Why does Jesus command the Demoniacs to say nothing? What is the point made by the quotation from Isaiah in §25 G Matthew?

   c) §26: What did Jesus do the last time he went off by himself? What is he doing here? (Note, this theme is not in Matthew.) What conclusion

31

does Jesus come to as to which is more important, healing or teaching?

d) §28: What is the man's illness? ("Leprosy" in Hebrew Bible can refer to a number of skin diseases, with psoriasis a high probability—see Bible dictionary, or Leviticus 14:3.) How was he healed? Why the command to go to the priests? (See Leviticus 13:49 and 14:2.) Why the command to say nothing?

5. General questions on healings:

a) What seems to be Jesus' attitude toward his healing activity?

b) What evidence is there, if any, of his deliberately choosing to make healing a part of his work?

c) Was his widespread fame as a healer sought by him, thrust upon him, or what?

d) What called forth his healing power?

6. If Jesus turned down miraculous powers in §20 (the temptations) how do you account for their appearance in his activity now, in these stories?

SECTIONS 29-33 *Records*   (52-54, 69-70 *Parallels*)
Overview: Development of Opposition to Jesus

The heading to Chapter V, Development of Opposition to Jesus, covers this material very neatly. In general the questions to be asked of each section are "What is the issue here?" and "How does Jesus deal with it?"

SECTION 29 *Records*   (52 *Parallels*)

1. Significant differences in text?

2. What is the Hebrew view of sin, its punishment and forgiveness? (See Deuteronomy 28:15; 21-22; 27-28; 58-62.)

3. What ailed the man? ("palsied" = paralyzed, in other translations)

4. Don't let the group discuss any of these big words— faith, sin, forgiveness—out of context. Ask always, What does that word mean *here*? If

you had no idea what the word meant, what meaning for it would you draw from this episode? (What does 'faith' mean *here*, for example? It means taking the roof off the house; it means eagerness, drive, determination, unstoppability.)

5. How does Jesus' statement to the man in D relate (if at all) to the purpose for which the man was brought?

6. Judging by the religious leaders' reaction, what did they hear Jesus as saying? What did he actually say?

7. In F how does Jesus relate forgiveness and healing? What meaning for the word "forgiveness" grows out of this episode?

8. "Son of man": meaning? Here the technique of asking for a minimum and a maximum is helpful. For Hebrew Bible references as to possible meanings, ask the group to look at Psalms 8:4 (simply humankind, or a human being), Ezekiel 2:1 and many other verses (the prophet himself; a person who is listening to what God says), Daniel 7:13 (generally taken as a Messianic reference, though I have never been able to see why it can't also be of the Psalms 8:4 variety). What would it mean to put each of these possible meanings into what Jesus says in G? Human beings—you and I—have power to forgive sins: the prophet has power to forgive sins; the Messiah has power to forgive sins.

9. On what basis could Jesus act and speak here with no feeling of irreverence or blasphemy?

10. In the context of this story, what is the meaning of "faith?" Of "sin?" Of "forgiveness?"

11. The source of healing lies where, in this story?

12. What does this story tell us about Jesus' concept of humanity? Of God? Of their interrelationship?

SECTION 30 *Records*   (53 *Parallels*)

1. Text differences?

2. Why could the Pharisees not associate with sinners? (See Leviticus 5:2-3.)

3. What lies behind defilement laws: fear; purity; or what?

4. Why could Jesus freely associate with sinners?

5. What is the source of F Matthew? What does it contribute to Jesus' argument?

6. What is the proper relationship of good and evil, according to the religious authorities? According to Jesus?

SECTION 31 *Records*   (54 *Parallels*)

1. Text differences?

2. For what are Jesus' disciples criticised in A? By what standards?

3. What is the point of B:

   a) as an image or parable, getting the point out of the whole story?

   b) if Jesus is equated with the bridegroom?

4. How can Jesus' position in B be stated without using the bridegroom image? What is he saying about the criticism in A?

5. What, if any, relationship is there between CD and AB?

6. Taking the image as a whole, not equating anything in the story with anything outside it, what is the point of the image of the "parable" in C? In D? In E?

7. In general, what are the three parables about? What, if anything, do they say about Jesus' estimate of his own message—its newness, its acceptability?

SECTION 32 *Records*   (69 *Parallels*)

1. Text differences?

2. What law were the disciples breaking in A?

3. On what principle was this law based? (Why the Sabbath? Take time for the group to look at Exodus 20 and Deuteronomy 5.)

4. What principle lay behind David's act in C? (I Samuel 21:1-6 and Leviticus 24:9; see footnote in Hebrew Bible references.)

5. What law or laws do we take as seriously and consider as central to our life today as the Hebrews valued the Sabbath law?

6. Why is F Mark not in Matthew/Luke? What is the meaning of F?

7. What do DE Matthew add to the Matthew account? What point do they make?

8. What is the meaning of the phrase "Son of man" in a) Mark? b) Matthew? c) Luke?

9. What point is Jesus making about the Sabbath in a) Mark? b) Matthew? c) Luke?

SECTION 33 *Records* (70 *Parallels*)

1. Text differences?

2. What is the attitude of the religious authorities?

3. How does Jesus become aware of this attitude?

4. What does D Matthew contribute to the argument? What point is Jesus making in DE Matthew? In E Mark/Luke?

5. Note "anger" in F Mark. Why not in Matthew/Luke?

6. Reaction of authorities in G. Why, in terms of this episode? Why, in terms of all the events and issues §29-33?

SECTION 34 *Records* (71 *Parallels*)

A summary. Not much to note except: How does Matthew see the activity of Jesus summed up in the Isaiah passage quoted in G?

SECTION 35 *Records* (72 *Parallels*)

In B, for what purposes were the disciples chosen? What characteristics of the disciples are hinted at in C?

SECTIONS 36-38 *Records*   (18-44 *Parallels*,
  Overview   Matthew; 73-78, Luke)

Don't read; leaf through pages, asking:

1. How much Mark in text? In footnotes?

2. What portions are common to Matthew/Luke? How much of the material?

3. As noted in parentheses, what are the lowest and highest sec-tion numbers of the Lukan material in italics?

4. Look at this portion (§80-114); describe the text situation there.

5. How much of §36-38 is in Matthew alone? (about half?)

The hope in all this work preceding is that it will begin to bring the Sermon on the Mount down out of the stratosphere by suggesting, at least, that what we have here are not reports of a specific discourse of Jesus, but different uses of and putting-together-of remembered and recorded sayings of Jesus. If this perspective doesn't emerge, you as leader should bring it out because the Sermon on the Mount needs to be brought down to earth before people can begin to work with it as living material, applicable to their lives, rather than as dead law laid on their consciences.

Explain that Matthew, and particularly the Matthew Beatitudes, are so familiar that it is hard to deal with them freshly, and therefore it is a useful exercise to forget temporarily that Matthew exists, and read the Lukan Sermon on the Mount (Sermon on the Plain, actual-ly, see §35 D) as if it were all we have.

SECTION 36 *Records*   (73- 74 *Parallels*)
  Lukan Sermon on the Plain

1. B: To whom is this sermon addressed?

2. B-I: meaning of "Blessed?" (Other translations are a big help here.)

3. J: What do the "woe"s add to the development of the idea?

4. What's good about being poor? What's bad about being rich? (Use "rich"

and "poor" in any and all areas of life, include money, brains, power, peace, security, and possessions of all kinds, inner and outer.) What's good about weeping? What's bad about laughing? Try to keep group from weighing in too heavily on the idea of *now* and *in the future*; that's a valuable insight, but not the final one, I think; in the final one, time is irrelevant.

5. What is the general territory covered by these "blessed"s: physical, political, economic, psychological, or what?

6. What state of being is Jesus here describing?

SECTION 37 H-R Luke *Records* (75 *Parallels*)

1. What is the connection, if any, with the preceding material in §36 B-J?

2. How would *you* describe the attitude Jesus describes in H-K?

3. What reasons does Jesus give in M-R for recommending this attitude?

4. According to Jesus, who benefits from the adoption of this attitude? (Stress this: *YOU* benefit, not the other person; this leads to a general question to apply to the whole sermon, both Luke now, and Matthew to come: How altruistic is Jesus' teaching here? With whom is he chiefly concerned, you or the people you are dealing with?)

SECTION 38 F-I, O-W Luke *Records* (76-78 *Parallels*)

1. What attitude is recommended in F? Why? What does it accomplish?

2. What (if anything) do the parables in GH add to the train of thought?

3. How close is the connection of thought between F and I? What does the parable, or image of the eye, in I add to the thought of F? Why the word "hypocrite" here?

4. Does Jesus condemn (or "advise against") the act of judging, the basis of judgment, or what, in F and I?

5. Is he requiring that one abandon all evaluation-processes? What else might he be requiring?

6. What is said about "goodness" in O-R? What point is made by the use of the tree/fruit image?

7. Meaning of U? How illuminated by the image in W?

8. In W, some kind of "doing" is stressed as important. What kind of "doing" is asked for in this discourse?

SECTIONS 36-38 *Records*   (18-44 *Parallels*)
Overview: Matthew Sermon on the Mount

It's assumed in the questions that follow that the group has already gone through the Lukan "Sermon on the Plain" (see §35 D) in §36–38. Now the focus is entirely on the Matthew material, with any Lukan comparisons to be made coming entirely out of the group's experience with that material.

Look through the whole very quickly, noticing where the breaks in the thought come. (The leader's guiding hand should be firm here; don't let them brood or make fine distinctions. You are just trying to get a rough idea.) If this were a theme and you were an English teacher trying to give it a grade, what would you say its general outline is? (What I would hope would emerge is that this is a highly structured, rather literary piece of work, with certain very well–defined themes which I would provisionally categorize as follows.)

SECTION 36 A-O *Records*   (19-20 *Parallels*)

1. Of the "Beatitudes," B-I, which do you find easiest to understand? (Use all translations available.)

2. Which do you find easiest to do? Which most difficult?

3. Is this material descriptive or prescriptive? If prescriptive, how possible is it to do the behavior by putting your mind to it? If descriptive, what state of being is delineated by these verses?

4. "Blessed": why? What reasons (translate as freely as possible) are given in the second half of each verse?

5. If there were a hole in the manuscript at all the points where the word "blessed" comes, what word would you put in, in the light of all the surrounding material?

6. K-O: What state of being is described? How do the two images of "light" and "salt" illuminate it?

SECTION 36 P-S through §37 A-R *Records*   (21-27 *Parallels*)
The Law

1. §36 P-S. Why would anyone think that Jesus had come to destroy the Law or the prophets? (Work out meaning in that time of those two words.)

2. "I come not to destroy but to fulfill": meaning of fulfill here? (It can be good to come back to this sentence after the group has done the whole stretch, §36 P through §37 R, and work out what this sentence has come to mean for them as a result of their work and also of their work on such passages as §30 through §33, esp. §32.)

3. In §37 A, what is Jesus setting over against the law against murder: another law; a statement of fact; or what?

4. What is the danger that he warns against in A? Who is harmed if it is not avoided? About whom does he chiefly seem to be concerned?

5. What does the parable full of legal imagery, in §37 B, add to the description of the "danger" in §37 A?

6. Ask questions 3 and 4 again about C. Work on the meaning of "lust"— what it means and what it does not mean. Use other translations. What does the vivid imagery of the right eye and the right hand add to the description of the situation of the lustful person?

7. DE provide a very incomplete picture of Jesus' thought on divorce, which is fully developed in §115. Ask group to draw a parenthesis around this material and save it for then. Incidentally, if you look carefully whenever there is Lukan material, it always reads more like a parenthetical insertion than as if it really belonged to the sequence of thought. Try it; you'll see. That's why I feel free to postpone D and E for consideration at its later appearances if the material is really distracting, as this is.

8. Don't take oaths: why not? According to §37 F verses 34 and 35? According to verse 36? "Of the evil one": what is dangerous to the person performing the act, about taking oaths? Why must it be simply Yes and No?

9. §37 G-J. What would you say for or against the standard in G? What is its value, if any?

10. How would you describe the attitude that Jesus sets over against this standard, in IJ? How, if at all, does this attitude benefit the person holding it? Try to keep the group from going off onto what it will do for the person on whom it is practiced. Jesus says nothing whatever about that, anywhere in this stretch of material, except in DE, which as I've said I consider an inter-

polation. It's worth emphasizing how completely his concern is for the person *doing* the hating, lusting, oath-taking, whatever—throughout.

11. L-R: What will it do for a person to take up the attitude that Jesus recommends in N? What is the "reward" that Jesus promises in Q? What reward does he promise in P?

12. What do these images of the sun and the rain falling on all alike suggest to us as to the nature of the Father? What do they suggest to us as to how we should treat other people?

13. What do you think of this whole idea of promising a "reward?" Are we not supposed to be "good" with no thought of "reward?" What seems here to be Jesus' attitude toward wanting/expecting a reward? (This theme will be developed more fully later, and especially in the material that follows, §37 TUY.)

14. R: What is R saying as a summary of L-Q? What does "perfect" mean in this context? (Use all translations and point out that Greek word translated here as "perfect" carries more the meaning, "completed," "fully mature.")

SECTION 37 STUY *Records*

In dealing with this stretch I do one of two things as a preliminary: either get the group to agree to postpone consideration of the Lord's Prayer to the Lukan setting; or if they want to do it now, draw a parenthesis around it temporarily, while looking at TUY, and look at it separately. This keeps the helpful structure of TUY (compare that of A-R) intact.

1. In all three instances—giving alms, praying, fasting—why does Jesus warn against public action? In "They have received their reward," what is the reward? Why is it harmful?

2. What do Jesus' images of secrecy in all three indicate as to the degree of secrecy he thinks necessary in the practice of these actions? Why does he consider it necessary?

3. What "reward" does he promise to those who do not seek the other "reward?"

If the group wants to do the Lord's Prayer at this point, then go ahead as follows:

SECTIONS 37 V-X, 85 A-D Luke *Records* (30, 146-148 *Parallels*) Prayer

1. Under what circumstances is this prayer given to the disciples according to §37 V and §85 A?

2. "Use not vain repetitions": How do we square this counsel with our frequent repetition of the Lord's Prayer? What is bad about repetition? What is good about it? What makes repetition "vain"?

3. "Your Father knows what you need": Then why ask him?

4. Why pray, according to §85 C? What does the story in C say to this question?

5. Why pray, according to §85 D? How do the father-and-child images illuminate this theme?

6. Compare §37 W and §85 B for different forms of the Lord's Prayer. Are there any significant differences?

7. Whose Father is the prayer addressed to? What does the father image of God say to us? (Note that there are many other images of God. See in the Hebrew Bible for instance, a "jealous" God, a "judge," a "ruler," a "creator," etc.) Does the father image help us or hinder us? (Consider an individual who has had a loving father, or a stern father, or a cruel father, or an absent father?) Why do we have to have *any* image of God? How do images help us? How do they hinder us?

8. Jesus speaks in §37 V and §85 CD of asking. How many things are *asked* for in this prayer? What kinds of things?

9. Which parts of this prayer seem most difficult to understand? Which seem most difficult to do? How much action is called for from us by the various phrases of this prayer? What kinds of action?

10. Only one portion of this prayer carries a condition — forgive. According to X, why is this? Is X a threat; a promise; a statement of fact; or what? (Compare §78 VW, if you are doing a skipping-around kind of consideration that develops one theme fully. Or if you are holding to continuity, simply say that there will be more on this later.)

41

SECTION 38 A-E *Records*   (32-35 *Parallels*)
Anxiety and security

Here again, invoking the principle that I mentioned earlier, I think you are free to postpone consideration of this material until you come to it in Luke. But if you and the group want to consider it here:

1. What is said about "treasure" in A? Is the idea of "treasure" in itself necessarily frowned upon? (Recall discussion of "reward" in §37 TUV.)

2. What is the main point made by the images of the eye and the slave? (The Greek word translated as "serve" carries much more the meaning "be a slave to.")

3. What reasons are given for not being "anxious" about the future, in D and E? What do you think of these reasons? How well, if at all, do they apply to life as we live it?

4. What do the images of the birds, the lilies, the grass contribute (if anything) to our understanding of Jesus' train of thought here? Are we being told to live in the present only, with no preparation for the future, no work done toward providing for our needs? How much "work" do those birds do? Those lilies and those grasses?

5. What conditions in our lives create our almost constant concern with the future? Under what ideal conditions could you imagine not being at all concerned about it? What connection, if any, do they have with the concept of God's kingdom, introduced in D, verse 33?

6. "O ye of little faith": What meaning for the word "faith" do you derive from its use in this section?

SECTION 38 F-J *Records*   (36-37 *Parallels*)
Judging

If you have done the Lukan Sermon first you've already looked at this and need only to review briefly in order to ask one question about portion J. If not:

1. Why not "judge," according to F? According to this who is harmed by the judgmental attitude warned against? What relation does this warning have, if any, to the thought in §37 X, considered earlier?

2. Are we being warned against all kinds of evaluation in this material? Or is a

distinction made, for instance in I, between "judgment" and simple evaluation?

3. What does the image of the eye and the "log" and "speck" (Revised Standard Version) contribute to this discussion of "judging" and simple evaluation? Is Jesus concerned about the whole act of judging, or with the standards by which we judge, or with what?

4. In J, what is Jesus warning against? What kind of evaluation is called for here?

SECTION 38 K-end *Records* (39-44 *Parallels*)
Miscellaneous Themes

1. K has already been looked at in connection with §37 VWX/85 CD. If not, postpone to Lukan point.

2. L, similarly, was looked at in connection with the Lukan §37 K. But if you want/need to look at it again, simply ask: How complete a standard is it? We usually think that it covers the subject, but does it?

> Little Willie, home from school,
> Where he'd learned the Golden Rule,
> Said, "If I eat up this cake,
> Sis won't get a tummy-ache."

3. M: Where elsewhere in this discourse do we find Jesus' thought relating to the "narrow gate?" To the wide gate? What does this image of a narrow or wide gate contribute to our thoughts on this subject?

4. N-T: What makes a prophet "false" according to N? What does the image of the tree and its fruit, P-S, contribute to this concept of falseness? (Try to work this out thoroughly, in preparation for later work on Jesus' use of the word "hypocrite.")

5. U-W: What two things are contrasted in U? What kind of "doing" is asked for in this discourse? How does this tie in, if at all, with the kind of "doing" for which "many" will want credit in V verse 22? What is Jesus' estimate of the "doing" described in verse 22? What does the image of the two builders in W emphasize? What is the single difference between them? What does this parable have to say about the importance of "doing?" "Doing" what, according to this discourse?

6. This is your chance to look back briefly, but tellingly, over the whole of the discourse.

SECTIONS 39, 42 *Records*   (46, 79, 83 *Parallels*)
Faith

Point out that the group has been looking at this word "faith" each time as if they had never seen it before and had no idea what it meant. Suggest that they continue doing the same thing in these two sections, except that they can, if they wish, use whatever sense of the word's meaning that they have built up from the group work on §29 D on the word, "faith."

Theme I: Meeting across cultural differences, §39 ABC

1. How would you describe a Roman official, that is, a member of the occupying force, who had done the things listed in A Luke: and who, in both versions, does not order, but sends to ask?

2. What is the captain's estimate of Jesus in B? What are all possible meanings of "Lord?" Is it a title of respect or what?

3. "I am not worthy": Why does the captain say this? Remind the group of Jewish pollution laws which discouraged Jews from associating with outsiders.

4. What does AB Matthew offer as a picture of the process by which two individuals of different cultures can meet each other genuinely and with respect?

Theme II: Faith, §39 BCE, §42 A-E

1. "A man set under authority": By what process does the captain come to understand Jesus' power? In the light of this process, how does he evaluate Jesus?

2. "I have not found so great a faith": Why is Jesus so impressed? How would you describe the captain's process of thought? What word would you apply to it? How does this word (whatever it is) relate to your understanding of the word "faith?"

3. What meaning would you give to the word "faith" in this context?

4. §42 is only in Luke; but mention §137 as a possible parallel.

5. According to the parable in C, which came first, love or forgiveness?

6. According to the application in D, which comes first? What, from

this incident and parable, would you take to be the relation of the two, love and forgiveness?

7. How would you describe the woman's attitude and behavior? How would you compare them with the captain's approach to Jesus in §39?

8. "Thy faith hath saved thee": In the context of this story, what meaning would you give the word "faith?"

9. Compare the man Simon here with the scribes and other religious authorities of §29 and §30. What do you see as their stumbling-block throughout?

SECTION 40 *Records* (80 *Parallels*)

1. Note text situation.

2. Any familiar elements to this story?

3. Would you say this was a miracle or an act of healing?

4. What moved Jesus to perform this act?

SECTION 41 *Records* (64-68, 81-82 *Parallels*)

Theme I: "Art thou he that cometh?"

1. "He that cometh" (A): What is the meaning of this phrase, as they ask it? (Compare §17 O Luke.)

2. What evidence thus far (and in which Gospels?) have we had of John the Baptist's relationship to and attitude toward Jesus?

3. What kind of "coming one" was John expecting according to §17 PQ?

4. Why does John the Baptist at this point raise the question if Jesus was the "coming one?"

5. Why does Jesus not answer the question in A directly? How does he answer it in C? What is the source of what he says in C? Where have we seen him using this quotation before? (§22 B)

6. What difference(s) do you see between the activities described in §17 PQ and those described in §41 C?

7. What does Jesus mean by "stumble" ("take no offense" Revised Standard Version) here? Why and in what ways might John the Baptist "stumble" concerning Jesus?

Theme II: John the Baptist

1. What points does Jesus make about John the Baptist in D? In E? In F? In G? (Don't stop to puzzle and analyze—just see what they are. Let the group work out meanings of these passages from the next questions.)

2. "Among them that are born of women" (E): In what ways, according to the text here, is John the Baptist great?

3. "He that is but little in the kingdom of heaven" (E) In what ways, according to the text here, is John the Baptist limited?

4. What is John the Baptist's relation to the kingdom of heaven/ God according to A-E? According to F?

5. What is said about John the Baptist in G? What connection with the Malachi quotation in E?

6. In the image of the children in the marketplace in I, what is said about the relationship of John the Baptist's general style and message to that of Jesus? What is said about the response that each of them meets? What is said about the responders?

7. "Wisdom is justified by all her children" (J Luke): meaning? What does this say about Jesus' attitude toward John the Baptist? How does it compare with the Matthew parallel?

8. H: This sentence appears frequently; what does it mean? What does it suggest as to the ease or difficulty of understanding the passage(s) in which it appears?

Theme III: "Woe unto Chorazin and Bethsaida"

K-Q are to be found elsewhere, later, in Luke. Save for then.

Theme IV: "Come unto me," R (68 *Parallels*)

1. A very famous teaching. Found in how many of the Gospels?

2. R: From what we've seen of Jesus' teaching so far, what are this

yoke and burden? Easy and light as compared with what?

3. "Meek and lowly": What light do previous teachings cast on the meaning of these words? On why Jesus describes himself thus? On why he thinks John the Baptist might stumble concerning him?

SECTION 43 *Records* (84 *Parallels*)

1. According to this passage, were there women among the general group of the disciples/followers?

2. What kind(s) of women?

3. What was their function in the group?

SECTION 44 *Records* (85 *Parallels*)

1. Where have we last seen Mark? What was happening in that section?

2. What opinion of Jesus is indicated here? Held by whom?

3. What basis is there for such an opinion?

4. Why is this passage not in Matthew/Luke?

SECTION 45 *Records* (85-88 *Parallels*)

Theme I: Preliminary observations

1. Note the two sources for this material: CEGIK based on Mark. ABFHJ and L-end based on Document Q.

2. Where is the Lukan version of this material placed in the Lukan text? What guides Matthew's placing of it here?

3. This is difficult material; hard to come to the heart of it. It will help to take portions not consecutively, but as they appear in first the Mark-related portions, then in the Document Q-related ones.

Theme II: The situation, A-H

1. What is happening in A? What is the reaction of the crowd in B? What is the reaction of the religious leaders in C?

2. How would you translate the imagery in C? What is the nature of this accusation?

3. What is Jesus' answer in E and G (the Mark-related material)?

4. What is his answer in F and H (the Q material)?

5. What about the attitude of the religious leaders does Jesus denounce in F? What is he trying to get them to see? "By whom do your sons cast them out?": What are the implications here as to the place of healing in the Hebrew tradition?

6. "If I by the spirit of God . . .": What estimate of Jesus' healings might grow out of an understanding of the first half of F?

Theme III: The sin against the Spirit, I-K, L-P

1. First look at K Mark to establish the fact that this mysterious sin is clearly linked very closely with what has gone before, that is to say, with whatever the religious leaders have shown forth as their attitude/reaction: "because they said, he hath an unclean spirit."

2. Note the contrasts in I and J. How far can one go in sin and blasphemy and still be forgiven? How far can one go in speaking against the Son of man? (i.e. Jesus? Or if not Jesus, who?)

3. What is the one thing that one cannot do and obtain forgiveness?

4. What in this context is the sin against the Spirit? (For this once, look over at the Gospel of John, §211 J, for the definition, "the spirit of truth.") What does this whole train of events, of argument and counter-argument, in A-H, have to do with truth?

5. What other possible meanings of the phrase "the Spirit/Holy Spirit" emerge from this section?

6. Why is this sin against the Spirit so serious?

7. "Hath never forgiveness" (IJK): why not?

8. L-P: What do L-O add to the thought? How does the image of tree and fruit apply to the issue here?

9. What is the meaning of P? How is it applicable here?

Theme IV: Signs, Q-V

1. What is the connection, if any, of Q-V with what has gone before?

2. Why do the leaders ask for a "sign?"

3. Why is it "evil" to ask for a "sign?"

4. What is the "sign of Jonah" according to S? According to UV?

Theme V: Unclean spirits, W

1. What sorts of human situations are spoken to here? What point is made about them?

2. What does W say about the whole concept of exorcism?

SECTION 46 *Records*   (89 *Parallels*)

For §46, see §49

SECTIONS 47,48 *Records*   (90-103 *Parallels*)
Overview: Parables of the Kingdom

What is a parable? Try to get the sense of the group working on this. Add your own definition, if you have one. (My own "working" definition is that a parable operates much like a joke, not stating but implying, with the punch part brought out at the end but contained in the whole and happening all at once.) The most important trait to focus on is the one-pointedness of the parable. When you come to the parables themselves, help the group to center on what one point the whole story seems to be making, and to resist the impulse to make an allegory of it, thus creating a running equation in which separate items in the parable are identified with separate items in the area where you are applying it—exercise this restraint in spite of §47 L-P where exactly that equation-making is done. Allegorizing (to my mind) can be fruitfully done later as a meditation on the material (as in §47 L-P) but for the group it is important to stay with the "one-pointed" idea.

I usually quote a sentence from an article on parables I once read: "In the parable, figure and idea touch each other at one principal point." I also quote a sentence from Sallie McFague's Speaking in Parables, *"If the listener or reader 'learns' what the parable has to*

(continued on next page)

49

'teach,' it is more like a shock to the nervous system than it is like a piece of information to be stored in the head." I also suggest as the best approach to a parable the question, "If this were a joke, what would be its point?"

And of course if the group can be brought to a point where their first reaction on reading a parable is the same kind of delighted joke-laugh at the neatness with which the point is made, you are in business! I often use Clarence Jordan's re-tellings of parables in his Cotton-Patch Matthew & Luke *for just this reason: they make people laugh.*

Theme: Why teach in parables?

1. What portions of §47-48 are neither parables nor explanations of parables? (§47 A, F-L, Q-V; §48 G-J, M,R,S.) What is the general theme of these passages?

2. Why teach in parables according to §47 G-K? (Note difference between Matthew and Mark/Luke.) Is Jesus saying that he is being deliberately obscure? If so, why?

3. Why teach in parables according to §47 Q-V?

4. Why teach in parables according to §48 I?

5. "Hearken" (§47 B); "who hath ears" (§47 FS, §48 M). "Take heed how ye hear" (§47 T): Why is there this frequent refrain? What does it have to do with the parable in §47 B-E? With §47 U-V?

6. "Unto you is given the secret" (§47 G): what secret? What seems in this material to be the differences between the disciples and "those outside?" What elements are necessary for the growth of understanding? (Compare §47 K and §48 R.)

7. What is one to make of Jesus' teaching technique as here presented? How does it compare with that of the Sermon on the Mount (especially the Matthew version)?

8. How does the parable of the good seed and the different kinds of ground it lands on speak to this whole matter of teaching and learning?

SECTION 48 *Records*   **(95-103 *Parallels*)**
The parables of the Kingdom

1. What is the subject of the parables in §48?

2. What were current concepts of the Kingdom as we have seen them? What were the ideas about how it would come: from the outside in; from the inside out; or what?

3. What are our concepts of the Kingdom and how it will come? (Try to get as many different ideas out on the table; encourage people to examine their unconscious or taken-for-granted assumptions, no matter how childish or inconsistent.)

4. Remind the group briefly of the one-pointed approach to parables. Ask them to keep in mind that these parables are designated as being about the Kingdom. And ask them to look at them freshly, without at the moment paying any attention to the interpretations in §47 M-P, §48 K-L, or §48 Q. Just respond to the parables freshly.

5. In each parable, §48 A-F, N-P:

    a) What is the point of the story *as story*? (No interpreting.)

    b) What point about the Kingdom is made in it?

    c) What old concept of the Kindgom is found in it?

    d) What new concept?

6. The interpretations in §48 K, L, Q stress which, the new or the old aspects of the Kingdom?

7. How would you summarize what Jesus is saying about the Kingdom: is the Kingdom inner; outer; or coming suddenly? Gradually? What is the cost of the Kingdom? Who or what brings it into being? Or does it come into being? Or is it always here?

8. What, if anything, is new in Jesus' teaching here?

9. Look at §48 R again, for a wrap-up, and compare §31 CD.

SECTION 49, 46 *Records*   **(89, 104 *Parallels*)**

This is also to be found at §46, and can be done there if that fits the class time better.

Theme I: The story

1. In D, what is Jesus' reaction to the arrival of his mother and brothers?

2. This account is an open-ended story. If you were completing it, do you think that Jesus (a) then went out to speak with his mother and brothers? (b) stayed with the crowd?

3. What do you think this story has to say about Jesus' relationship to his mother and brothers?

4. What is Jesus doing to family relationships here: dismissing them; reevaluating them; transcending them; or what?

Theme II: The saying

1. What is Jesus' definition of brother, sister, mother? In §46 Matthew/Mark? In §49 Luke? Compare also §87. What are the similarities? What are the differences?

2. Which of these definitions is most meaningful to you? Why?

Theme III: The will of my father/of God

1. The will of God is: specific actions; a set of standards; or what?

2. What attitude does loyalty to the will of God involve: living in accordance with laws; or ideals; laying aside one's own will entirely; or what? In §20 how did Jesus go about finding what God wanted him to do?

SECTIONS 50-54 *Records*
Overview: The place of faith in the work of Jesus

It is good to remind the group of the work they have done in establishing a meaning from the text of the meaning of the word, FAITH. Remind them of §29 D, and §39 and §42, if it is appropriate; all very quickly. Then continue.

SECTION 50 *Records* (105 *Parallels*)

1. What does B Matthew contribute to the account? (Note Lukan placing elsewhere.)

2. "He (Jesus) was asleep" (D): How do you account for this behavior in the middle of a "great storm?"

3. In §29, §39, §42, Jesus has responded very favorably to people who turn to him in need, and has called their action "faith." Why does he, then, question the disciples' doing the same thing?

4. "O ye of little faith"; "Have ye not yet faith?"; "Where is your faith?": What are the differences in tone and direction of these three sayings? What general area do they bracket? What is Jesus calling the disciples' attention to in their own attitude?

5. Faith in what? Faith that what? What does the kind of faith that Jesus demonstrates have to do with whether or not death comes to them in this storm?

6. Where was there "a great calm": in the sea; or the disciples; or both?

7. What content would you give to the word "faith" in this section?

SECTION 51 *Records* (106 *Parallels*)

Use Mark with excursions as needed into the other two.

1. Remind the group of the work done on first-century theories of mental illness (in the §24–§28 stretch) as set alongside our own theories. What ailed the man, in twentieth-century terms? "We are legion" (G): meaning?

2. What do you make of the swine episode (H-I) in terms of the first-century concepts of mental illness? In terms of ours?

3. What did the demoniac do that opened up for him the possibilities in GM? What was Jesus' part in the healing?

4. M: Heretofore Jesus has told people to say nothing. Why does Jesus now tell the man to go home and tell his friends? What is the difference between what Jesus tells him to say and what he actually says?

SECTION 52 *Records* (107 *Parallels*)
A story within a story

Theme I: The story of Jairus, A-B, L-U

1. "The child is not dead but sleepeth" (P): Is this a statement of physical fact or a statement about death in general; or both?

2. "Tell no one": Jesus returns to the usual pattern. Why does Jesus ask this?

3. Why is there so down-to-earth a conclusion as U, after all the drama of the incident? What is Jesus' attitude toward this event?

Theme II: The woman in the crowd, C-J

1. What was the woman's ailment? What is Hebrew law concerning women with "issues of blood?" (See Leviticus 15:25-28.) What taboos did the woman have to overcome in order to touch Jesus' robe? Why was she afraid when Jesus began to ask who had touched him?

2. How did Jesus know that she had touched him? Where have we had other implications that Jesus felt drained by his ministry? How does the Matthew account deal with this particular theme? (F-I)

3. What is Jesus' attitude toward the woman?

4. What content would you give the word "faith" in this section?

SECTION 53 *Records* (56-57 *Parallels*)

1. What are the familiar elements in this healing story? What new ones, if any?

2. "According to your faith": What is Jesus' part in this healing?

3. What content would you give the word "faith" in this section?

SECTION 54 *Records* (108 *Parallels*)

The Lukan story was looked at in the Lukan context, §22, so focus on Mark/Matthew.

1. What estimate of Jesus is expressed in C?

2. What estimate in D?

3. "And they were offended in him": Why is it difficult to recognize outstanding qualities in someone whom you have known, and whose family you know? Why were they put off by him? Because of his family? Because of what he was doing?

4. How would you interpret or translate Jesus' comment in H? With what or whom is he equating himself in this passage?

5. Mark says in J: "And he *could* there do no mighty work." Why not? What, if anything does this say about possible limits to Jesus' power? Have we met any other suggestions of possible limits? (What about §52 F?) What are the implications of this passage?

6. Matthew says, "And he *did* there not many mighty works." Why not? What are the implications of this passage?

SECTION 55 *Records*   (58 *Parallels*)

Are there any new features in this report of Jesus' activities?

SECTION 56 *Records*   (109 *Parallels*)

Theme I: The calling of the disciples, §56 A-D

If you have not considered this material at the §35 A-C point, pick that material up at this point and ask the following questions of both sections:

1. What preceded Jesus' appointing the disciples/apostles according to §56 AB? According to §35 A?

2. What is the meaning of the word "disciple?" Or the word "apostle?"

3. For what purposes or duties were the disciples/apostles appointed, according to §35 B? According to §56 C? (Look at each version, Matthew/Mark/Luke.)

4. §56 D, §35 C: How much can we find out about the disciples from the incidental references in this list? What does the nick-

name Peter, or "Rock," tell us about Peter? What does the nick-name "Sons of thunder" tell us about James and John? Are Andrew and Philip Jewish names or Greek names? What is a "Canaanean," or as the footnotes say, "Zealot?"

Theme II: The mission of the disciples, §56 E-M

1. To whom does Jesus send the disciples according to E Matthew? (Compare §57 F Matthew.) To whom does he send them according to Mark/Luke, up to now? (And compare §57 B.)

2. F: What are they being sent out to do?

3. How are they to proceed according to GH? According to I? According to J? According to K? According to M?

4. What would these ways of going about a mission accomplish? What would they prevent? What kind of atmosphere would they create around the people who were practicing them?

5. How good a summary of G-L do you find in M?

SECTION 57 *Records*   (59-63 *Parallels*)

This material is found at this point only in Matthew. It is much better to hold this material until the Mark/Luke point, which deals with it in a final-crisis setting, a more suitable setting than this beginning-of-the-mission spot. But pick up on §57 R and §59, for the wind-up of this mission; and ask of §59, what is Jesus' chief concern for the disciples here in Mark?

SECTION 58 *Records*   (110-111 *Parallels*)

Herod and the daughter of Herodias. This is essentially a Hebrew Bible or folk-tale sort of story about keeping an oath that should never have been made in the first place (compare the story of Jephthah in the Hebrew Bible) and really needs nothing more than reading and noting the details. So no special questions. But before that, look at §58 A-C. What is Herod's evaluation of Jesus?

SECTION 60 *Records*   (112 *Parallels*)

Theme I: Importance of this story

1. How many times does this story appear in the three Gospels? (three times here; two more times at the §67 point; once in John, at §178.)

2. Are these separate events, or retellings of the same story? What does the absence of Luke at the §67 point indicate as to his opinion on this matter (if anything)?

3. Whether separate events or re-tellings, what does the reappearance of the theme indicate as to its importance?

4. Why was this story so important to the early church? Why is it important to us? What is/are its meanings and overtones?

Theme II: The story

1. Go through the story, making the details vivid and trying to enter into it. If you were a disciple, for example, what would be the effect on you? If you were a member of the crowd, what would be the effect on you?

2. What are all the possible explanations of the multiplication of the loaves and fishes?

3. All the previous miracles have involved making some change in the minds or bodies of human beings—a situation which is not so hard for us (cf. psychosomatic medicine) to understand. What about our modern grasp of the physical laws of the universe concerning matter? How do they affect our ability to understand this miracle?

4. What is the meaning behind this event? What modern events, if any, does it call to your mind? What recurrent Sunday-morning event? (If that isn't a leading question, I don't know what is. But the Eucharistic echoes deserve to be brought out, especially in the light of the details in G.)

SECTION 61 *Records*   (113 *Parallels*)

Theme I: In the midst of the sea

1. What immediately precedes this event? (Look at §60 JK, and §61 A.)

2. Why did Jesus send them away without him?

3. Note that this material is not in Luke. How many sections before we meet Luke again? What sort of material is in these sections?

4. What do the disciples make of the event in B? How does Jesus handle their fear? What is their reaction in D Matthew? In D Mark?

Theme II: Jesus and Peter, C Matthew

1. Why could Peter walk on the water at first? When and why did he stop being able to walk on the water? What experiences have you had, if any, of doing something directly and almost unconsciously, and then suddenly being unable to continue? What went wrong?

2. "O thou of little faith": Why does Jesus say this to him?

3. What meaning or content would you give to the word "faith" in this section?

4. "They understood not concerning the loaves": What does the event in §60 have to do with this? What were they to understand concerning the loaves?

SECTION 62 *Records*   (114 *Parallels*)

1. What are the familiar themes on this recurring subject of healing?

2. What are the new themes?

SECTION 63 *Records*   (115 *Parallels*)

This is a hard section to unscramble, partly because Matthew and Mark arrange it differently; and partly because the whole "Corban" bit in H Mark is not all clear as it appears here. The Revised Standard Version is clearer, and though I haven't checked it out, I would imagine that some of the new translations would be clearer still. And a Bible Dictionary would be some help.

Theme I: Argument with the religious leaders, A-H

1. What is Jesus being criticized for in B and C? Is the current practice of the Hebrews founded on law or tradition, according to the text?

2. What point does Jesus make about tradition versus law in C-F Matthew and F-H Mark?

Theme II: Defilement, I-L (Refer back to ABC)

1. What concept of defilement is presented in ABC?

2. What concept of defilement does Jesus' saying, in I, present?

3. Why were the religious leaders offended by it?

4. How does Jesus develop his concept of defilement in KL?

Theme III: Jesus' teaching technique

1. With whom is Jesus dealing in D-H? By what method does he teach, or try to teach them?

2. By what method does Jesus teach the multitudes in I?

3. How does he teach the disciples in JK?

SECTION 64 *Records*   (116 *Parallels*)

Theme I: Insiders and Outsiders, "Jew" and "Gentile"

Use Mark first.

1. What is Jesus' position in DE? What do you think of the image he uses? In what way do you think he is using it? Is it to be taken as a whole, commenting on the insider/outsider situation; or using "dog" as a specific reference to the woman; or what?

2. In either case, how does the woman respond? What do you think of her response? How would you have responded?

3. Why, in F, does Jesus seem so pleased with her response?

4. What has happened to Jesus in this exchange?

Theme II: The Matthew account

1. What differences, if any, do you find in tone, development, effect between these two accounts?

2. What seem to you to be the words, phrases, sentences, which create this difference?

3. What is the difference in the effect that the two stories have upon you as you read them? Think carefully to keep them separate from each other. It's not easy; we have lumped them together for centuries.

SECTION 65 *Records* (117 *Parallels*)

This is fairly routine. No questions.

SECTION 66 *Records* (117 *Parallels*)

1. Another healing. What are the familiar features?

2. What new features, or unusual ones are there?

SECTIONS 67-69 *Records* (117-120 *Parallels*)
Overview

Several things deserve noticing about this stretch. One is the absence of Luke from §61 through to §71. What theories, if any, might you come up with as to why this is so? Another thing to notice is a kind of circling-round in (earlier) §60 through §62, and here §67 through §70, of the same set of themes: feeding a multitude; a night-sea journey with the disciples; a reference to not understanding "about the loaves"; and a healing.

SECTION 67 *Records* (118 *Parallels*)

Look back at §60. What are differences? What are similarities? Is this a different event? Or another telling of the same story? What is the meaning of this event? (See questions on §60.)

SECTION 68 *Records* (119 *Parallels*)

1. See questions on the similar account in §45 Q-V. This is an important incident, appearing in §45, here, and later in §88; and the whole business of seeking signs takes on an importance at various points later. So it might be worthwhile to ask again the questions asked of §45 Q-V, with the addition here of:

2. What does B Matthew contribute (if anything) to an understanding of Jesus' position on "signs?"

SECTION 69 *Records* (120 *Parallels*)

1. A: What does Jesus mean when he warns the disciples against the leaven of the Pharisees?

2. B: "We have no bread": What do the disciples think Jesus is talking about when he refers to the leaven of the Pharisees?

3. What is Jesus' reaction to their comment?

4. What point is he making about bread?

5. What point is he trying to make about the leaven of the Pharisees?

6. What happened to/in this dialogue, anyway?

SECTION 70 *Records* (121 *Parallels*)

1. Another healing. What are the familiar features?

2. What new ones?

SECTIONS 71-74 *Records* (122-124 *Parallels*)
Overview

With §71 through §74 you come to what I think is the heart of the first three Gospels. If I had a total of four sessions with a group, in which to present the Gospel message, I would choose this material.

Because of its depth and importance, I usually try to slow down the pace of the group when they are working on this material, and make them look harder and more closely at it than they have done before with anything except maybe the Baptism and Temptations. This is particularly true of §73 AB on which I try to spend one whole session if I can get away with it—which doesn't happen often.

SECTION 71 *Records* (122 *Parallels*)

The themes of §71 are so closely interwoven that it is hard to separate them, but here's a try:

Theme I: The Messiah/Christ

1. Judging from previous work on the texts, what did the term *Messiah*, or Anointed One, and its literal translation into Greek, *Christ*, mean to the general public of first-century Palestine? (§4 C, §9 A, §10 CD, §11 BC, §17 PQ)

2. What clues, if any, do we have as to what the term meant to Jesus?

3. What evidence, if any, have we seen of Jesus' publicly proclaiming himself to be the Christ?

4. What evidence, if any, have we seen that Jesus saw himself as the Christ?

Theme II: Jesus charting his course

1. Why does Jesus ask the question in B? For the disciples' sake? For his sake?

2. What estimate of Jesus does the answer in C give?

3. Why does Jesus ask the question in D? For the disciples? For himself?

4. If the questions in B and D are to be considered as helpful to Jesus, in what way or ways? To what extent do the answers in C and D meet his needs? To what extent do *we* need feedback from other people to know who we are, or how to chart our course?

5. What does Peter's answer imply as to Jesus' power, his mission, the course his life will take, according to the usual concepts of the time as to what "the Christ" will be and do?

Theme III: Jesus and Peter, EF

Note that E and F are only in Matthew; and note also that this is one of only two places where the word "church" appears in the Gospels (cf. §78 S) and both are in Matthew.

1. "Blessed are thou, Simon": why? What are all possible meanings (maximum/minimum) of the material that follows?

2. What does this insight mean for Simon? For Jesus?

3. "My father has revealed it to you": In what other ways might the insight have come to Simon?

4. Why does Jesus give Simon his new name at this point?

Theme IV: Silence

1. Why does Jesus in all three texts, tell the disciples not to proclaim this insight publicly, or in fact to anyone?

2. Where and when have we seen Jesus asking for silence before?

SECTION 72 *Records* (122 *Parallels*)

Theme I: The Messiah/Christ

1. "Son of man": To what extent is this a Messianic title? (cf. Daniel 7:13-14)

2. "Son of man": To what extent is Jesus referring to himself?

3. What is Jesus saying in A about what is going to happen to the Son of man (Mark/Luke), himself, (Matthew)? How close is the future he predicts to the general expectation of what the career of the Messiah will be like?

4. Note the many versions of this prediction at the bottom of the page. Which is the most detailed? Which is the least detailed? How do you account for these variations?

Theme II: Jesus charting his course

1. What leads Jesus to see this kind of future for himself?

2. What Hebrew Bible precedents are there for it? (cf. especially Isaiah 53)

Theme III: Peter's response

1. Why is Peter so resistant to the future that Jesus sees? How many of his taken-for-granted beliefs does it upset?

2. How do we react when our cherished or taken-for-granted concepts and beliefs are upset? Find instances of such personal upheavals, large and small (small ones are often the most illuminating).

Theme IV: Jesus and Peter

1. Why does Jesus condemn Peter's reaction so strongly?

2. "Thou mindest not the things of God, but the things of men": meaning?

3. "Blessed art thou, Simon" (§71 E); "Get thee behind me, Satan": What do you make of two such diametrically-opposed statements one coming right on the heels of the other? How could Peter change so? Or is it a change?

Theme V: The Messiah/Christ

Through the dialogues of §71 and §72, what is happening to Peter's concept of the Christ? To our concept of the Christ? Of power? Of glory?

SECTION 73 *Records*   (123 *Parallels*)

General notes: Pick up and review from §71–72 the whole theme of how one finds out what one is and can do, and how one expresses in the world what one is—how we "become what we are"—as this theme is stated and worked out in this development of Jesus and his relation to "the Christ."

§73 A and B seem to me to be picking up, not just for Jesus, but for all of us, the question: What is the place for denial and loss in our own life-process of becoming what we are?

A good first step is to look at the saying in A (all forms including those in the footnote) to note:

1. *how important a saying it seems to be, judging from its number of appearances;*

2. *what is its simplest and more direct form;*

3. *what different settings it appears in, alone or linked, as here, with the material in B.*

Theme I: Jesus' attitude toward the self, A

1. What does it mean to deny oneself?

2. What is the difference, if any, between denying oneself and deny-ing oneself something?

3. What is Jesus' attitude toward the self, as we've seen it up to now? (Look back at the Sermon on the Mount, and point out that we have a relevant saying to plug in here, "Love your neighbor as yourself" §130 M.)

4. In A Luke "deny oneself" is commended. Why then would "lose oneself" be condemned in B Luke?

5. "Take up his cross": meaning? In Luke it is "take up his cross daily": meaning? How does this compare with that of Matthew/ Mark?

Theme II: Ends and means, B

*Confusion of **result** with **process**: or the whole clutch-and-possess technique we tend to apply to the **process** that is life.*
    First point to this as the Great Paradox—so-called in many

discussions of this material. And talk a little about what a para-dox is; ask the group what they think it is. What does a paradox do? (The Zen koan, a kind of Eastern paradox, is designed to confuse the mind and stop the top-level intellectual processes, in order to make way for a deeper kind of response.)

Then look at the different versions of the saying and come to rest on the simplest form: §112 Luke (footnote), which has no "sake," but is paradox pure and simple.

1. In the first half of the saying, which is *process* and which is *result?*

2. In the second half, which is *process* and which is *result?*

3. Failure here comes from confusing what two things? What is the sound *process?* What is the sound *result?*

4. Is this true in life as we observe it? Do we lose what we clutch at and try to possess? What are some aspects of "life" that we clutch at? Work in as many areas as possible—money, family (especially our relations with our children), intellectual attain-ments, ideas, concepts, social position; you can go on and on getting the group to consider new areas.

5. How do/can we begin to let go of this false and unproductive approach to life?

6. Looking back over the whole consideration of §73 AB, what is the threat, or the promise, or the statement of fact, here?

Theme III: "For my sake," BCD

1. Go back and pick up the thread of "for my sake" in other ver-sions of B as well as the simple one already considered. Examine all possible meanings.

2. Take CD as picking up the "for my sake" theme. Examine the dif-ferences in the three texts.

3. What is said in C about one's fidelity to Jesus? Is the statement a threat; a promise; a statement of fact; or what?

4. "When the Son of man comes": meaning? (Work for more than simply "at the end of the world.") "Come in glory": meaning? Is this experience anything accessible to us now? Individually or collectively?

5. What is said about this coming in D? Coming of what, in D?

Section 74 *Records*   (124 *Parallels*)

Theme I: The experience, and the growth in insight, of the disciples

1. Whose experience is this, as here described?

2. What is the nature of the experience in BC? What is its content or message? What is the meaning of the presence of Elijah and Moses with Jesus?

3. How does Peter interpret the BC experience, in D?

4. How is the BC experience developed and/or corrected in E?

5. Why "tell no man" in I?

6. What do the question and answer in K-O contribute to the disciples'/our understanding of this episode?

7. What is Jesus saying about "Son of man" (meaning whom?) by means of the Elijah-John the Baptist analogy?

8. "How is it written" (L): where? In the Bible? In the laws of the universe? Where?

Theme II: The "Little Resurrection"

The whole question here is what this episode says as a summary and development of the theme of gaining and losing life, first, for the Messiah, §71–72, and everyone/us, §73.

1. What, if anything, does §74 have to do with the theme of "losing life" that is developed in §71–73?

2. "After six days": We have seldom met a stress on time in these accounts; e.g. "straightway" in §20 A, and a few others. What significance if any do you attach to this?

3. What in general do you make of this "mountain-top" experience?

4. What does Jesus say about it in I?

5. Some commentators have referred to this as "the little resurrection"; what do you think of this term?

67

SECTION 75 *Records*   **(126 *Parallels*)**

What are the text differences? (This, though I don't mention it every time, is the first question for each section. Handle it quickly, but firmly. A group will bypass it if possible.)

Theme I: The Disciples

How are the disciples doing on their own? Recall the sending-out in §56.

1. Whom is Jesus rebuking in C?

2. What do you make of Jesus' reply to the disciples in G? Compare §50 E and G. What is Jesus expecting of them?

3. What does the image in H add to the thought here? Compare §48 E.

Theme II: Jesus' dealing with the father of the boy, D Mark

1. "If thou canst do anything": How does Jesus respond to this?

2. "All things are possible to him that believeth": In what sense, if any, do you find this true?

3. In what way, if any, does the phrase "him that believeth" restrict the clause "all things are possible?"

4. "I believe, help thou my unbelief": meaning?

5. What meanings of the words "faith" and "belief" grow out of this episode for you?

SECTION 76 *Records*   **(127 *Parallels*)**

Note significant differences among the texts.

Theme: The disciples' lack of understanding

1. "They were afraid to ask him about this saying" (C Luke; compare Mark): Why afraid? What saying? What was so hard to understand about it, in its Lukan form? (B Luke)

2. Compare B Mark. What was hard to understand about that saying?

68

SECTION 77 *Records* (128 *Parallels*)

Comment on "half-shekel"; Revised Standard Version has "half-shekel tax," other translations say simply Temple tax.

Theme I: Obligation and freedom

1. What is the point made by Jesus in A, verse 25? (This passage is translated in many ways, but the Greek is definitely "sons" and "strangers" and it is worth puzzling over those terms.)

2. "Therefore the sons are free": Free *from* what? Free *to* what? (A reference back to "sonship" in §18 and §20 can be helpful here.)

Theme II: Fulfilling outer requirements

1. Why does Jesus instruct Peter to pay the tax?

2. How essential is the element of miracle in B to the point of this episode?

3. In the light of this whole episode, how would you describe Jesus' attitude toward payment of the Temple tax?

SECTION 78 *Records* (129-136 *Parallels*)

A long and varied section, with many interwoven themes, nearly all of which appear in better—that is, clearer and easier to work out—contexts in other sections. If I am in any kind of hurry, I simply pass over A-Q and pick up R-W. But if there is time, it is good to look at the whole for another perspective on the material—always keeping in mind that the material does not need to be gone into deeply, because it has been or will be seen in other contexts.

Theme I: Greatness, A-G

1. How does Jesus answer the disciples' thinking in A?

2. What is the meaning of this reply in B Mark? In E Matthew? In H Luke?

3. What point is Jesus making about greatness? About children?

Theme II: Inclusion

1. What is the point made by I? Compare §45 H. How do these two situations differ?

2. In the light of the two situations, how contradictory do you find the two sayings?

Theme III: Little ones, H-Q

1. Note text situation.

2. Who are the "little ones?" Compare §57 Q.

3. What is Jesus' chief concern about these "little ones?"

4. Why is the "stumbling" theme (LM) in here?

Theme IV: Forgiveness

1. Note text situation.

2. Note the unusual word "church" in S. Compare §71 E. (Note text situation.)

3. Compare T, here, with §71 F. Here addressed to whom?

4. S: How characteristic is this material of Jesus' teaching as you have seen it up to now? What about U?

5. How closely are R and V related in Luke? How consecutive is their train of thought?

6. What point is made about forgiveness in RV, Matthew/Luke?

7. What is the focus of the parable in W: the king; the servant; or what?

8. What point is the parable making? What does it add to R-V?

9. What general attitude is recommended in §78 toward the young, the tentative, the newly-planted, the lost?

SECTION 79 *Records*   (137 *Parallels*)

This is simply a progress passage and needs no real comment, beyond possibly noting "steadfastly set his face" in Luke. Read it and move on.
    Between §79 and §80 is one of two places (the other is the Matthew

Sermon on the Mount) where you might assign homework, though even here it isn't necessary. But if you want to, ask the group to read, at home, very quickly and not studiously, §80–114, or the equivalent in their Gospels (Luke 9:52–18:14) and come to class prepared to discuss the impression it made on them.

SECTIONS 80-114 *Records*   (137-186 *Parallels*)
Overview: The "Hard Sayings"

From here on for quite some time you will be working with Luke alone, with some cross-references to Matthew in italics in Sharman. My procedure in these questions is going to be simply to note and pass by those sections that the group has already dealt with in the Matthew setting. For your part you can do whatever seems indicated by the group's needs—read, and pass on; read and pause to note and discuss differences in the two texts; pause for full discussion or re-discussion.

If the group has read Sections 80 through 114 rapidly, ask them to sum up their reactions to the material. If the words "harsh," "hard," "difficult," etc. don't come up, fish for them. It's important to notice a real difference of tone in this stretch.

1. If you feel a difference in this material, how do you account for it?

2. What do you make of it?

SECTION 80 *Records*   (137 *Parallels*)

Theme: Intolerance and prejudice

1. Why didn't the Samaritans receive Jesus? (See John 4:9; Ezra 4:1-4; II Kings 17:24-28; Bible dictionary.)

2. What precedent is there for the disciples' idea of revenge? (See II Kings 2:23-25.)

3. What causes prejudice, in the light of all this?

4. How is a person or a group to deal with opposition and rejection, according to Jesus here? Compare §56 K.

71

5. (Refer to Footnote 3.) "Ye know not what manner of spirit ye are of": How to describe this spirit? How to overcome it?

SECTION 81 *Records* (138 *Parallels*)

1. Do the settings of these three sayings help or hinder us in considering them?

2. All three are stated poetically, in images. What point is the image of the foxes and the birds making? The image of the dead? Of the plough?

3. What (if any) central state of mind do these three images point toward?

SECTION 82 *Records* (139-142 *Parallels*)

Portions A through I are considered at the Matthew point, §56. But note differences, e.g. A and D.

Theme I: Mighty works, and rejection, J-R

1. "Kingdom of God is come nigh": meaning?

2. "That day": meaning?

3. "Mighty works": meaning? What light does R cast on this?

4. What is Jesus' evaluation of these "mighty works" in R? Compare §38 V.

Theme II: Jesus' Prayer, S-U

1. What is the mood of this prayer? What is its content?

2. "These things": what things?

3. How do T and U develop the meaning and mood of this prayer?

SECTION 83 *Records* (143-144 *Parallels*)

Theme I: The process of the dialogue in AB

1. "What shall I do?" Why not "What must I be?" Why should the lawyer think that he has to *do* anything?

2. How does Jesus deal with the lawyer's questions?

3. From where does the lawyer get his answer in verse 27?

4. "Desiring to justify himself": meaning? How does his question "justify" him?

Theme II: The Great Commandment, verse 27

Save detailed work on this for § 130 LM. But you could ask:

1. Where in the Hebrew Bible is this from?

2. How good a summary of the Ten Commandments is it?

Theme III: Question, B, and answer, CD

1. What question does Jesus actually answer? (Suppose you had CD, reconstruct B.)

2. Why did he not answer the lawyer's question directly?

3. What point does the parable in C make about the whole subject of having and/or being a neighbor? How does this point relate to the lawyer's questions in A?

4. Why did the Samaritan stop, not the priest or the Levite? How does this relate: a) to times when we might have stopped to help in a situation, but didn't; or b) to times when we have been able to respond as needed?

Theme IV: Interiorizing the story in C

This is an approach that some groups enjoy and find very helpful. It involves looking at the story as an interaction between parts of oneself—asking who is the wounded traveler in us, the priest, the Levite, the Samaritan. It also involves seeing, in terms of this story, how parts of us help or hinder other parts of us. Another story that lends itself to this approach is §29, the paralyzed man. But it depends on you and the group—try it and see how it goes, or if you feel uneasy with it, don't do it.

SECTION 84 *Records* (145 *Parallels*)

Theme I: One thing needful

1. Is this story about housekeeping?

2. What is the "one thing needful?" Imagine the situation reversed: Mary fretting because Martha isn't sitting and listening—what light does this exercise cast on "one thing needful?"

Theme II: Jesus and women

1. Jewish women in Jesus' day (and today in Orthodox and Hasidic Judaism) were not supposed to concern themselves with religious and intellectual matters. Their place was working with Martha. In the light of this, what do you make of Jesus' attitude toward Mary in this story?

2. This story, like the parable in §83 C above, lends itself well to being "taken inside." Who is the Mary in us? Who is the Martha in us? How do these two sides of ourselves treat each other? What does Jesus have to say to this inner conflict (if there is one)?

SECTION 85 *Records* (146-148 *Parallels*)

Questions on this material are to be found at the Matthew point, §37 vwx.

SECTION 86 *Records* (149 *Parallels*)

Questions on this material are to be found at the Matthew point, §45.

SECTION 87 *Records* (151 *Parallels*)

See also §46 and §49.

1. What is Jesus saying about family relations here?

2. "Hear the word of God and keep it": meaning? What relation, if any, to earlier material studied? (I'm fishing here for a look back at §38 uvw, but if it doesn't come, leave the group with the question and pass on.)

SECTION 88 *Records*   (152 *Parallels*)

Questions on this material are to be found at the §45 Q-V point. It takes a bit of work to get the group away from simply dismissing the "sign of Jonah" as the miracle that Matthew describes in §88 C, and over to look-ing at what the sign of Jonah is in the Lukan context here, where the three-days theme is not even mentioned. So I suggest:

1. Tell briefly the story of Jonah, or read selected items, recommending that group members read the whole at home. Stress the humor of the story, and the reluctant-prophet theme; *and* the fact that the people of Nineveh listened to the message and took it to heart. No "what sign do you show us" stuff.

2. With all that under their belts, then the question, again, is: What does Jesus mean by the "sign of Jonah" here?

3. What is meant, in the light of all this, by C Luke here?

4. Why, then, is Jesus so critical of "this generation," in B?

SECTION 89 *Records*   (153 *Parallels*)

Text comparison.

Theme: Inward light

1. What is Jesus saying in this Lukan passage about "the light that is in thee?"

2. How do these eye/lamp images help (or hinder) his develop-ment of the theme?

3. To what extent is the "light that is in thee" under your control?

4. What kind of light in you can be darkness? How could this condi-tion come about? What can be done about it?

5. Compare §45 I-K. What relation, if any, do you find between "light" and "Holy Spirit?"

SECTION 90 *Records*   (154 *Parallels*)

There is a fuller and even more devastating treatment of this subject at the § 132 Matthew/Mark point. Save for then.

SECTION 91 *Records* (155 *Parallels*)

Various elements of this section have been dealt with at the points listed in parentheses in the Matthew column, or will appear at the § 134–136 point. Read, comment on generally, and move on.

SECTION 92 *Records* (156 *Parallels*)

Theme I: "It isn't fair!" A

1. What is asked of Jesus here?

2. How does Jesus deal with the question? With the man?

Theme II: Wealth

1. What point is the parable in B making

   a) purely as a story?

   b) as a comment on wealth?

2. What does C add to the point made by the parable?

3. How close is the connection between A and BC?

4. "Rich toward God": meaning?

SECTION 93 *Records* (157 *Parallels*)

Questions on this are to be found at the Matthew point, §38 A-E.

SECTION 94 *Records* (158-159 *Parallels*)

Save for the § 136 point. But look at EGH, ask for comments and questions.

SECTION 95 *Records* (160 *Parallels*)

Theme I: Inner tensions

1. "A baptism to be baptised with": What are the various possibili-

ties as to what Jesus means here? What is his attitude toward this "baptism?"

2. "Fire upon the earth": meaning?

3. "Peace in the earth?": What does Jesus mean by this?

4. How would you describe the feelings expressed in these images?

Theme II: Outer tensions

1. Across what lines do the divisions in B cut?

2. Why does Jesus think he brings division, not peace?

SECTION 96 *Records*   (161 *Parallels*)

If possible, try to do §96 and §97 in the same session.

Theme: "This time"

1. Both A and C are in Matthew in other settings, §68 B, §37 B. What theme do these passages develop in this setting?

2. "This time": meaning what? Jesus himself, his activites and teachings? The religious conditions of the time? The Roman occupation?

3. "Hypocrites": Have the group remind themselves of the meaning of this word as used through the earlier material (§37 TUY and §38 I, for example). How would this state of mind keep one from understanding "this time?"

4. What particular warning does Jesus give in C about the dangers of "this time?" (Note to leader: the destruction of Jerusalem, in the year 70 A.D., generally supposed to have occurred before this Gospel was written, may give special point to these sayings.)

SECTION 97 *Records*   (162 *Parallels*)

Theme I: Events of "this time," §96 A

1. A: What kind of offense would bring so severe a Roman attack?

2. B: What particular significance, if any, is there to this "tower": military; occupation duty; or what?

Theme II: Meaning of events

1. "Sinners . . . offenders": against whom?

2. "Except ye repent": of what? "Ye shall all likewise perish": how and why?

3. C: What is the central point of this parable? What is its application here?

4. Is Jesus counselling what would nowadays be called "collaboration"; Or what?

SECTION 98 *Records*   (163 *Parallels*)

A healing story.

1. How valid is the objection in B?

2. What is Jesus' defense?

SECTIONS 99-100 *Records*   (97-98 and 165 *Parallels*)

These sections are covered at the Matthew points indicated in parentheses in text.

SECTION 101 *Records*   (169, 170 *Parallels*)

Theme: The work of Jesus

1. Compare Jesus' description of his work in A with that of §41C.

2. How would you describe his work as he sees it?

3. "The third day I am perfected": meaning? ("Perfected" is the same Greek word as in "Ye must be perfect," Matthew 5:48; and it means much more than "perfect" as we understand the word. It means "fulfilled—completed—brought to maturity—finished"—and more; it has all kinds of overtones.)

4. "It cannot be that a prophet perish out of Jerusalem": why not? What would be a modern equivalent for what Jerusalem represented to first-century Hebrews?

5. What is Jesus' self-estimate in A?

6. What is Jesus' feeling about the city to which he is going, in B?

SECTION 102 *Records*   (168 *Parallels*)

A healing story, similar to §98.

1. What is the accusation?

2. What is Jesus' defense?

SECTION 103 *Records*   (169-170 *Parallels*)

Theme I: Greatness

Within this feast situation of A, what is Jesus saying about greatness? Is he condemning greatness itself; or a certain way of trying to gain it; or what?

Theme II: The Feast

1. What does the feast setting of C and of the parable in E-H suggest as to the nature of the Kingdom of God?

2. "Recompensed in the resurrection of the just": how? How does this "recompense" compare with that of §37 TUY?

3. What point does the parable in E-H make about the feast? Who decides whether or not the invited guest is actually present?

SECTION 104 *Records*   (171 *Parallels*)

Theme: "Don't start anything you can't finish."

1. What do you make of the word "hateth" in B? How much and what is covered by the things that must be "hated?"

2. "His own cross": meaning?

3. What point is made by the two images or parables in D?

4. Is Jesus trying to discourage followers; or what?

5. What is the point of E in this context, if any? (cf. §36 KL)

SECTION 105 *Records* (172-173 *Parallels*)

Theme: Relation of righteous to sinners, compare §30

1. What is the situation in which these parables were spoken, in A?

2. What is the point of the parable in B?

3. What is the point of the parable in C? How do B and C apply to the situation in A?

4. In terms of the setting in A, where is the major focus of the parable in D: on the wandering son; on the stay-at-home son; on the father?

5. What is the problem confronting the elder brother? What guidance, if any, does the father give him in handling it?

6. This is another good parable for "taking inside." Who is the wandering son in us? Who is the elder brother? Who is the Father in us? Or, how do we meet the father in us?

SECTION 106 *Records* (174 *Parallels*)

Theme I: Cleverness, shrewdness

1. What is the point of this parable?

2. "He had done wisely" (verse 8): in what way?

3. What is said here about "the sons of the light?" Who are they?

Theme II: Faithfulness

1. How close is the connection of verse 9-12 with the parable? With one another?

2. What does each saying mean, taken as a separate saying? What questions about "faithfulness" and "mammon" does each one raise, and what answer, if any, does it give?

SECTION 107 *Records*   **(176 *Parallels*)**

This has already been done at §37–38. But look at it briefly to see what connection, if any, its themes have with § 106.

SECTION 108 *Records*   **(177 *Parallels*)**

Theme I: Reward and punishment

1. What is the point of this parable? If there seem to be two points, where is the dividing line?

2. According to this parable, what determines one's fate in the future life?

Theme II: Repentance

What is Jesus saying in verses 26-31 as to what brings about repentance? What will fail to bring repentance?

SECTION 109 *Records*   **(178-180 *Parallels*)**

This material was previously done in §78 and §75.

SECTION 110 *Records*   **(181 *Parallels*)**

What is the point of this parable? "Unprofitable": why?

SECTION 111 *Records*   **(182 *Parallels*)**

This is a fairly standard healing story, and a good opportunity, if you want to use it, to review the elements of the Gospel healings. What familiar elements here? What new ones, if any?

SECTION 112 AB *Records*   **(183-184, verses 20-22 *Parallels*)**

Save C-M for § 135.

Theme: The Kingdom

1. The inquirers ask *when* the Kingdom of God is coming. Jesus' answer focuses on what?

2. "Comes not with observation": meaning?

3. "The kingdom of God is within you": meaning? What does the alternate reading in the footnote add to this meaning?

4. What equation, if any, do you find between "kingdom of God" in A and "days of the Son of man" in B? What are all possible meanings of the phrase "days of the Son of man?"

SECTION 113 *Records* (185 *Parallels*)

1. What is the meaning of the parable? To what other parable is it similar (§85 C)?

2. "His elect": Have we met this phrase before? What is its meaning: for the early church; for us?

3. Verse 8, "when the Son of man cometh": meaning? What relation to "days of the Son of man" (§112 B)?

SECTION 114 *Records* (186 *Parallels*)

Theme: Righteousness

1. Assuming that what the Pharisee says of himself is true, what's wrong with the stance he takes here? (cf. §110)

2. Meaning of "justified": Why does the publican's attitude produce this result?

3. What is the point of this parable?

4. Is B (verse 14) a threat; a promise; a statement of fact?

SECTION 115 *Records* (187 *Parallels*)

Theme I: The Law

1. How does Jesus deal with the question in A?

2. "For your hardness of heart . . .": What is implied here as to Jesus' position on the divorce law?

3. Does Jesus hold the same view of all laws? (cf. §37 A-F, §31-33)

4. What (if anything) in Jesus' view is prior to law?

Theme II: Marriage and divorce

1. "Whom God hath joined . . .": In what way or ways does God join a couple together?

2. In D, what is Jesus formulating: a law; a principle; or what?

3. Under what conditions do two people make the kind of "one" or "one flesh" described in D?

4. Under what conditions do they fail to make this "one?"

5. What is Jesus formulating in F? Note differences in texts.

6. G: Why and when is it "not expedient to marry?"

7. In G verse 11, does the phrase "this saying" refer back to F; or forward to G verse 12; or both?

8. What inner or psychological states does the "eunuch" image point toward? What is said about the marriage relationship here?

SECTION 116 *Records* (188 *Parallels*)

Theme I: Nature of the kingdom of God

1. "Of such *is*": What indication here as to whether the Kingdom is of present time; future time; or what?

2. What indication here as to its nature?

Theme II: Children

1. What are children *really* like? Name all the characteristics you can think of, "good" and "bad."

2. What, if any, of these characteristics would make the Kingdom of God accessible to them?

3. What things are accessible, in our familiar everyday life, to children that aren't easily available to adults? What have we lost?

4. Compare Jesus' other statements about entrance into the Kingdom: (§36 B; §48 N-O; §81 BC; §100 C; §103 D-H; §112 A; §117 GI).

5. What does this episode tell us about the nature of the Kingdom? About Jesus' attitude toward children?

SECTION 117 *Records*   (189 *Parallels*)

Theme I: Goodness, AB

1. What are differences in the text between Matthew and Mark/ Luke?

2. What is Jesus saying about himself in B Mark/Luke? What is he saying about "goodness" in general?

3. What are the differences between "goodness" in B; "eternal life" in A; and "treasure in heaven" in E?

Theme II: Jesus and the seeker, C-F

1. What is covered by the first of commandments in C? What dimension is added by Jesus' addition in E? Why the specific injunction to this particular person here, rather than the general one in §83 A?

2. How good a general precept is this in E? Where (if anywhere) have we found it elsewhere in Jesus' teachings?

3. How would you describe Jesus' dealings with this seeker?

Theme III: Jesus and the disciples, G-J

1. Why were the disciples astonished?

2. "Then who can be saved?" (Who, indeed?) Why not? What is Jesus' answer to this question?

Theme IV: Jesus and Peter, K-N

1. What is the general principle of life outlined in M? In what sense is it true, if at all?

2. What do L and N contribute to this principle? How consistent are they with the thought of M?

SECTION 118 *Records*   (190 *Parallels*)

Theme I: The laborers

1. What did they all have in common?

2. Why, at pay-off time, were the laborers first hired so angry? How justly?

Theme II: The Master

How does he deal with the complaint of the laborers? What do you think of his reply?

Theme III: The parable

1. What is the point of the story *as a story*?

2. What point is it making about the Kingdom of heaven/God? What (if any) other parable(s) does it remind you of?

3. What does B contribute, if anything? (cf. §117 N) What connection, if any, between §117 and §118?

SECTION 119 *Records*   (191 *Parallels*)

Theme : Predictions

1. How specific are these predictions? Compare other predictions in §72 A, §76 B, §112 D.

2. How well do the disciples understand these predictions?

SECTION 120 *Records*   (192 *Parallels*)

Theme I: The text

1. Where is this material in Luke?

2. Differences between Mark and Matthew? What is their effect on the story?

Theme II: Greatness

1. "On thy right hand . . ." (B): What kind of "glory" or Kingdom do John and James (or their mother) seem to be expecting?

2. What is Jesus' response to this desire for greatness?

3. "Cup . . . baptism": What does Jesus mean?

4. G, compare §117 L: Which seems more characteristic of Jesus' thought as we've seen it?

5. What is Jesus' concept of greatness as stated in §120 IJK?

6. How in general would you describe Jesus' way of dealing with the request in B: rebuking; encouraging; or what?

SECTION 121 *Records*   (193 *Parallels*)

1. What is the literary effect of having (Matthew/Luke) the healing of the blind follow §120's difficult teaching on greatness, and §119 G Luke references to disciples' lack of understanding?

2. Differences among texts? (Matthew/Mark/Luke)

3. C: What estimate of Jesus does "son of David" express?

4. What causes the healing according to Mark/Luke? According to Matthew?

5. "Thy faith hath made thee whole": Then what is Jesus' function in the healing, if any?

SECTION 122 *Records*   (194 *Parallels*)

Text situation? Note vivid details in verses 1–4.

1. What are the steps of the process here? Who makes the first advance?

2. "Publican" or taxgatherer = "sinner": why?

3. "The half of my goods" etc. What changes on Zacchaeus' part are involved here?

4. How does Jesus respond? Why does he not insist on "*all* my goods" as in §117 E?

5. "Salvation is come to this house"; "that which was lost": What was the loss, what is the salvation in this story?

SECTION 123 *Records* (195 *Parallels*)

Text situation? This story is found in another setting in Matthew. What is the setting here?

Theme: The Kingdom

1. "They supposed the kingdom of God was immediately to appear": What sorts of expectations about the Kingdom are implied here?

2. What does the parable (B-I) say concerning these expectations— particularly "immediately?"

3. What does the additional (compare Matthew) theme of C and L add?

4. What does this story imply as to Jesus' ideas about how and when the Kingdom comes? Compare with earlier stories, §48 and with §112 A.

SECTION 124 *Records* (196-198 *Parallels*)

Theme I: The colt episode

1. How did Jesus know the colt would be there?

2. Why did Jesus want to ride into Jerusalem? Why not walk as usual?

3. What is the meaning of this ride, according to C Matthew?

Theme II: Hosanna!

1. Who are these multitudes in FG?

2. What is the maximum/minimum meaning of what they say in G?

3. Who are the multitudes in J Matthew?

4. How does their estimate of Jesus square with the one in G?

Theme III: Jesus' reaction (HI Luke, verses 39-44)

1. "Rebuke your disciples": for what?

2. "The stones will cry out": meaning?

3. How would you describe Jesus' attitude toward the events in FG?

4. What is Jesus' state of mind in I? "Wept": why?

5. "The time of thy visitation": meaning?

6. "The things that belong to peace": What were they then, what are they now, in your estimation?

SECTIONS 125, 127 AB, 127 CDE *Records*   (199, 201 *Parallels*)

Theme I: The Fig Tree

1. What (if any) is the logic of Jesus' attitude toward the fig tree?

2. What is the fig tree an image or symbol of:

    a) in Jesus' thought (cf. §97 C)?

    b) in Hebrew thought (cf. Hosea 9:10; Jeremiah 24)?

3. What relation, if any, does this episode have to the events of §124?

4. How similar is Jesus' state of mind here to that described in §124 HI Luke?

5. What do you make of the fig tree's withering, §127 B?

Theme II: Power, faith and prayer

1. What did the disciples make of the fig tree's withering?

2. What, if any, is the connection of §127 CDE with §127 AB? What kind of comment is CDE on AB?

3. What is the relation of faith to power (C)?

4. What is the relation of prayer to power (D)?

5. What is the relation of forgiveness to power (E)?

SECTION 126 *Records*   (200 *Parallels*)

Theme: Symbolic act (cf. §124, §125, §127 AB)

1. What had brought about the state of the Temple described in A?

2. What was Jesus objecting to about this state? Why "robbers?"

3. What (if anything) could he hope to accomplish by his act in A-C?

4. How spontaneous an act is it? How violent? How does it square with the picture of Jesus that we've formed up to now?

5. What were its results?

6. "For they feared him": why?

7. "Every night he went out of the city": why?

SECTION 128 *Records*   (202 *Parallels*)

Theme I: Authority

1. How would you re-phrase the question in A?

2. Why is it important to the Jewish authorities?

3. Why does Jesus not answer this question directly?

Theme II: Obedience

1. What relationship does Jesus' question in B have, if any, to the question asked of him in A?

2. How would you describe the mental processes outlined in CD?

3. Why do they not answer Jesus' question?

4. Why does Jesus not answer theirs?

SECTION 129 *Records*   (203-205 *Parallels*)

Theme: Authority and obedience

1. A (203 *Parallels*): What point does this parable make?

2. How is this parable allied (if at all) with Jesus' questions about John the Baptist in §128 B?

3. What light does this parable cast on the meaning of the word "repent?"

4. What does the parable in C-G (204 *Parallels*) say about authority and obedience? What is its point, taken simply as a parable? What is its point if Jesus is equated with the son of the owner?

5. Two images of stones in H-J: What do they say about the Jewish leaders? "They perceived that he spoke of them": why? Why do they react as they do?

6. What is the point of the parable in L-O (205 *Parallels*), within this context of dialogue with the authorities?

7. What is the point of the parable in P? What is its relation to L-O? (Compare Lukan version of L-O in §103 E-H.) (170 *Parallels*)

SECTION 130 *Records*   (206-208 *Parallels*)

Theme I: Tribute, A-D (206 *Parallels*)

1. "Spies . . . catch him": how and why?

2. "Is it lawful?": lawful from what point of view? Is this a religious or political question?

3. How would you describe Jesus' answer: a smart evasion or something more?

4. What point or points is Jesus making in his answer? How closely related is his answer to the situation in which he finds himself?

5. Why does Jesus answer this question and not the one in §128 A? (202 *Parallels*)

Theme II: Life after death, E-K (207 *Parallels*)

1. How would you re-phrase the question of the Sadducees in F?

2. With what points about life after death does Jesus answer it?

3. How would you paraphrase what Jesus is saying about life and death in GH? What he is saying about resurrection?

4. "Not the God of the dead but of the living": meaning?

5. In these passages is Jesus restricting conjecture to this life; making a statement about future life; or what?

Theme III: Summary of the Law, §130 L-Q (208 *Parallels*)

1. What is the difference in the two situations, Matthew/Mark versus Luke? (Compare §83 A; 143 *Parallels*.) What is the difference between Matthew/Luke and Mark?

2. What ideas are peculiar to Mark in this section? What do they contribute to this episode?

3. "Tempting him": Why is this a trick question?

4. What are the sources of Jesus' reply in M?

5. How adequate a summary of Hebrew law is this?

Theme IV: Love, §130 M

Here is a great place to use a technique that is sometimes most helpful—to discuss this passage pretending that there is a hole in the manuscript wherever this word "love" appears. (This can be very useful with all the large vague Biblical words that we all think we know the meaning of. As the Zen Buddhists would say, "Empty the cup!")

1. What could you put into that empty space where the word "love" is temporarily absent? Supply words, phrases, whole sentences. Keep in mind that whatever you choose must fit all three relationships—to God, neighbor, self.

2. How obey-able is a command to love?

3. What is the relationship of love and the law?

SECTION 131 *Records* (209 *Parallels*)

Theme: The origin of the Christ

1. What point is Jesus represented as making here? A simple point of lineage?

2. To whom was this question most obviously important? To Jesus, or the early church?

3. How much concern has Jesus shown up to now as to the origin of the Messiah?

SECTION 132 *Records*   (210-211 *Parallels*)

Note: Since this is probably the single passage in the first three Gospels most offensive to Jews as representing an unhistorical and very unfavorable picture of the Pharisees, it is important to begin translating the term immediately. There are many possibilities—"hypocrites"; "holier-than-thou"; rigid legalists; "pillars of the church." What I would advance as a general statement of the subject is:

Theme: Warnings against destructive religious attitudes

1. "To be seen of men": reminiscent of what earlier teaching?

2. What attitudes and actions are described in B-E? What might be their modern equivalents in the religious circles we know?

3. FGH: What is the contrasting attitude here recommended?

4. Is H a threat; a promise; or what?

5. In each "woe" I-R, what fault of organized religion or professional "goodness" is here described? What modern forms of each are we familiar with: in churches; politics; our knowledge of ourselves?

6. What light do all these instances cast upon the meaning of the recurrent word "hypocrites?"

SECTION 133 *Records*   (212 *Parallels*)

This story, like several others (e.g. §46, §49, §83, §87, § 125, § 127 A) can be examined very usefully as if it were a parable by looking for the one point of the story and then examining the implications of that point.

1. What point does Jesus make from his observation of the widow's gift?

2. How does this point apply to giving in general?

SECTIONS 134-136 *Records*   (213-229 *Parallels*)

This material goes very well taken quickly, in a lump, and digested slowly (we hope) as time goes on. It represents material that was very important to the early church, a fact indicated by its presence in Mark—the only full-length discourse to be found in that Gospel. As the many section-divisions in Parallels *indicate, it is a collection of material about many different aspects of the future—a literary putting-together, which cannot very easily or usefully be considered as a talk given by Jesus on some one occasion.*

Theme I: Text situation

1. What are the text relations in §134 (213-216 *Parallels*)? In §135 (217-224 *Parallels*)? In §136 (225-229 *Parallels*)?

2. Which Gospel presents the fullest treatment of this theme at this point in the text?

Theme II: The Future

1. What is the situation described in AB? (Try to imagine the effect upon you of being told what the disciples are told in B, while you were admiring the Capitol building in Washington, for instance.)

2. "When shall these things be?" What things: according to Mark? Luke? Matthew? What different aspects of the future can you distinguish here?

3. "The sign of thy coming"; "The end of the world" (note alternative translations of the Greek in the footnotes): meaning?

4. What kind of future is described in D-F? How well does it fit into any of the aspects of the future suggested by C? A "future" confined to the first century? Or more general? What is said about it at the end of F Matthew/Mark?

5. What kind of future is described in F-N? What is represented here as being Jesus' chief concern about it? Where else in Matthew does this material appear?

6. What kind of future is described in O-S? (See especially O Luke.) What is Jesus' chief concern about it?

7. What kind of future is described in §135 A-E? What is Jesus' chief concern about it?

8. What kind of future is described in G-H? (Note numerous Hebrew Bible references.)

9. How do these different futures fit into the categories distinguished in question 2 above?

Theme III: Attitude toward the future

1. §135 L-S: What is Jesus' advice to the disciples (and to us)? Work on full meaning of the word "Watch." Note different Luke ending.

2. For each of the following parables, ask the question, "What kind of ' watching' does this parable describe?" §135 PQ Mark; §136 AB; §136 C(D); §136 E-G; §136 H-P(Q); §136 S.

Theme IV: General comment

How does this discourse strike you? How would you compare it to the Sermon on the Mount, for instance?

SECTION 137 *Records*   (231-233 *Parallels*)

For background on the Passover and the feast of unleavened bread, probably all that is needed at this point is a brief reference to Deuteronomy 16:1-3, 5-6, 16, bringing out the fact that there was a great gathering at Jerusalem at this point.

Theme I: Jesus' impending arrest

1. In what we've seen up to now, what had Jesus done and taught that might make the authorities want to put him out of the way?

2. "Not during the feast": why not? "By subtlety": why?

3. F: What reasons can you suggest for Judas' betrayal of Jesus to the authorities? Why would a member of the group closest to Jesus want to do this?

Theme II: The woman's extravagant gesture

1. What is the situation in B into which the woman comes?

2. What is the disciples' reaction to her act? How appropriate to what Jesus has taught them?

3. What is the issue here in C, stated generally? What modern instances of the same issue can you find?

4. What is Jesus' response to the woman's action? How related

   a) to the basic issue?

b) to the disciples' reaction?

c) to the woman?

Section 138 *Records* (234-237 *Parallels*)

As general preparation, spend some time looking at Exodus 12:21-27 for the meanings underlying the Passover observance; at Exodus 24:3-8 for the Covenant; at Leviticus 16:20-22 for the concept of the Scapegoat.

Theme I: Preparation for the Passover, A-C

"A man bearing a pitcher of water": Is this prevision, or pre-arrangement? Compare Matthew's account.

Theme II: The Betrayer, D-F

1. "As it is written" (DE): where? (See Isaiah 53.)

2. EF: How would you describe the response of the disciples?

3. "Thou hast said": meaning?

Theme III: The Last Supper, G-J

1. GH Luke: What are the tone, feeling and content of Jesus' actions and sayings in this passage? What are all the possible levels at which he is speaking?

2. "I will not eat . . . I will not drink henceforth": meaning?

3. "Until it be fulfilled in the kingdom of God": meaning?

4. IJ: What are all possible meanings of this action

    a) as derived from readings in Exodus and Leviticus?

    b) for Jesus?

    c) for the disciples?

    d) for us?

5. Discuss each one of the "until"s at the end of G, H, and J. What do they say to you? What was Jesus experiencing? What was its relation to the Passover feast?

95

6. What do bread and wine symbolize to you, if anything? What is common between them, and what different?

Theme IV: Greatness, L-N Luke

1. What is the text situation? In what setting is this material found in Matthew/Mark? How appropriate is it there?

2. How appropriate is it here? Why worry about precedence at this point?

3. What two definitions of greatness are contrasted in M?

4. "I appoint to you a kingdom"; "Ye shall judge": how and why? What does this imagery say to you?

SECTION 139 *Records*   (238 *Parallels*)

Note that there are two stories here, Matthew/Mark on the one hand and Luke on the other, and that the Lukan account is not on the way to Gethsemane, but at the Last Supper. The general approach, as always, is to note significant differences among the texts.

Theme I: Shepherd and flock, A-D Matthew/Mark

1. "Offended/caused to stumble"; "be scattered abroad": how and why?

2. How integral a part of this conversation is C? How relevant is its content?

3. How do the disciples (especially Peter) respond to Jesus' prediction? What makes them so sure that they will not deny him?

Theme II: Simon/Peter's function, B-D Luke

Note "you/thee" of B, a distinction that is hard to preserve in modern English. What is the distinction made here?

1. "When thou hast turned again": meaning? Turned from what?

2. "Stablish thy brethren": meaning? Establish/strengthen in what?

Theme III: Instructions for the future, E Luke

1. Why this change from the instructions in §56?

2. "Buy a sword": How consistent with Jesus' teachings and general attitude up to now?

3. "It is enough": meaning? (Check different translations.)

4. "That which concerns me hath fulfillment": what? Where written?

SECTION 140 *Records*   (239 *Parallels*)

Note that, as throughout most of this last portion of the account, Luke's version is different.

Theme I: Finding the will of God, B-G Matthew/Mark

1. "Greatly amazed ... sore troubled ... sorrowful unto death" (B): What are all possible reasons for (and levels of) Jesus' reaction here?

2. "This cup": What are its contents? What are the major elements of the situation, outer and inner, that confront Jesus here?

3. What courses of action are still open to Jesus at this point?

4. What are the steps of Jesus' process in discerning the will of God for him at this point? (Be sure you start at the beginning, with Jesus being quite clear what *he* would like. We tend to overlook that.)

5. "What thou wilt": What does Jesus find out as to what God's will for him is at this point? How does he find it out? When? Does he ever get a definite answer? If so, what is it?

6. EFG: Why does Jesus repeat the process three times? What development, if any, of his thought is there in each of the three times?

7. What is the function of Peter, James and John in this section?

8. E: What temptations are met by the disciples in this section? By Jesus?

Theme II: The Lukan account, A-E

1. What are the differences in tone, atmosphere, and effect of this

account? How does the picture of Jesus in it compare with that of Matthew/Mark?

2. By what additions, subtractions, changes are these differences brought about?

SECTION 141 *Records*   (240 *Parallels*)

Theme I: Judas, B

1. B: Why this need for a sign? What do you make of this particular sign?

2. "Friend . . ." (Matthew); "Betrayest thou the Son of man . . .?" (Luke): What difference is there in the portrayal of Jesus' attitude as shown here?

Theme II: Use of force, E-H

1. What does E Luke add to the episode of the swords in DE?

2. What does F Matthew add? Compare §139 E Luke.

3. "That the scriptures might be fulfilled": what scriptures? How? "Thus it must be" (F Matthew); "Thus": how? "It": what? "This is your hour and the power of darkness" (Luke): meaning?

4. Judging from these three phrases and from the whole of §141, how would you describe Jesus' attitude toward what is happening? What relation does this attitude bear to the inner struggle shown in §140?

SECTION 142 *Records*   (241 *Parallels*)

Note significant text differences and in the placing of the events in sequence and in time.

Theme I: Peter's denial

1. When does Peter's denial take place in Matthew/Mark, before or after Jesus' first trial? When does it take place in Luke? What effect, if any, would such a difference have upon Peter's reactions?

2. Why does Peter deny that he is one of Jesus' followers? What are the pressures upon him?

3. "I will not deny thee" (§139 D): What has happened to Peter since then?

Theme II: Jesus' first trial

1. When does this trial take place according to Matthew/Mark? According to Luke? What difference, if any, does this make in the development of the account? In the legality of this first trial?

2. What is the accusation against Jesus in C? Why does Jesus not answer it?

3. What are the implications of the question or command in E Matthew/Mark? What are the implications of the two-part question N-O Luke?

4. Why does Jesus answer this question?

5. How does he answer it? "Thou hast said" (Matthew); "I am" (Mark); "If I tell you . . . If I ask you . . . Ye say . . ." (Luke): What differences among these replies?

6. What part of Jesus' reply is similar in all three? What are all possible levels of meaning for this saying about "Son of man?" (Son of man meaning in Hebrew Bible usage three possible things: a human being (see Psalms 8:4); a prophet (see Ezekiel); the Messiah (Daniel 2:1).

7. Why does Jesus' answer condemn him in the eyes of the authorities?

SECTION 143 *Records*   (242-247 *Parallels*)

Theme I: Judas, B Matthew

1. Compare Acts 1:18. How do you account for this difference?

2. What clues if any, have we had in the texts, so far as to Judas' motivation in his betrayal of Jesus?

3. "I betrayed innocent blood": innocent of what?

4. Reactions of priests, "What is that to us?" Compare Jesus' attitude toward Zacchaeus in §122.

5. Why did Judas hang himself? What is the difference between his reaction to his own guilt, and that of Peter in §142 K?

Theme II: Jesus' second trial

1. C Luke: How good a summary is this of Jesus' activity up to now?

2. "Thou sayest": Compare §142 E Matthew and O Luke. What kind of answer is this?

3. Why does Jesus not answer in E? Why does Pilate marvel at this?

4. FGH Luke: What is the course of events here? What is Herod's attitude toward Jesus? What does this episode add to the account?

5. How would you describe Pilate's attitude toward this trial in I KM? What do J and L Matthew contribute to the account? N?

6. What are all the pressures impinging upon Jesus during these two trials? How would you describe his response to them?

SECTION 144 *Records*   **(248-250 *Parallels*)**

Theme I: Famous "seven last words "

1. Where is each one to be found? (1 in G Matthew/Mark; 3 in CEH Luke; 3 in §217 EFG John.)

2. How much overlap of the seven among the four accounts?

3. Since the accounts clearly differ, follow the two Synoptic variations, first Matthew/Mark, then Luke, separately.

Theme II: Jesus' Crucifixion, A-H Matthew/Mark

1. What are the implications of A as to Jesus' condition?

2. What are all the things impinging on Jesus in CDE? (Compare §37 I.) What are the pressures and stresses upon the self/Self (compare also §73 AB) of these events? How does Jesus meet them?

3. What is the significance of what Jesus says in G? What state of

mind does it indicate? From what is it quoted? (Read Psalms 22.)

4. Judging from this material, and from H, how would you say Jesus met his death?

Theme III: Jesus' Crucifixion, A-H Luke

1. What is the meaning of the saying in B? What is Jesus' area of concern here?

2. What is the meaning of the saying in C? What is Jesus' area of concern here?

3. What is the meaning of the saying in E? What is Jesus' area of concern here?

4. What is the significance of what Jesus says in H? What state of mind does it indicate? Quoted from what? (Look at Psalms 31.)

5. How would you describe Jesus' death in Luke? How would you compare it with the Matthew/Mark account?

Theme IV: Other people at the Crucifixion

Pick up details in I-L, all three accounts.

What is the significance of the details in this material?

SECTION 145 *Records* (251 *Parallels*)

Theme: The Burial of Jesus

1. Joseph "boldly went in and asked for the body of Jesus" (B): Why was boldness necessary? What elements of Joseph's position made this action possible?

2. Why should Joseph ask for Jesus' body? Why didn't the disciples?

3. "Pilate marvelled if he were already dead": why? (Compare §144 H.)

4. What do you make of the fact that only the women among Jesus' followers are mentioned as present at the crucifixion (§144 L) and the burial (§145 F)? What clues does this fact give

as to the disciples' state of mind at this time? (Compare §142 H-K, and §139 BD.)

SECTIONS 146, 148 *Records*   (252 *Parallels* and page 188)

1. "That deceiver said": when? to whom? How likely would such a saying have been to become generally known?

2. "Lest his disciples . . . steal him away": Who, first of all, needed evidence that Jesus had risen? Why would the disciples want to remove Jesus' body from the tomb?

3. "And the last error (*fraud*, Revised Standard Version) will be worse than the first": meaning?

4. In §147 D Matthew "the watchers did quake." Why are there no watchers in the Mark/Luke accounts?

5. How important is the empty tomb as a proof of the resurrection of Jesus

   a) to the priests and elders in §148?

   b) in the Gospel accounts?

   c) to us?

6. What are all possible explanations of the empty tomb?

SECTION 147 *Records*   (253 *Parallels*)

Theme I: Text relationships and general situation

1. Note the footnote to §147 G, also the note on Mark 16:20 Revised Standard Version. What are the general limits of Mark's original record?

2. How parallel are the accounts of Matthew/Luke in the material following §147 G Mark?

3. Where else have we found a similar situation with regard to parallelism? (Compare Sections 1-16.)

Theme II: The Empty Tomb

Note: In this and all the other material dealing with the resurrec-

tion of Jesus, the questions are basically, "What is described as happening here?" and "What is the meaning of this event, or this detail?"—not, "Do we believe this happened?" That's a matter for the individual to decide after all the happenings have been looked at: after "What happened?—What's its meaning?"

1. Who rolled away the stone according to Matthew? Mark? Luke? What possibilities occur to you other than those mentioned here?

2. What did the women see when they entered the tomb according to Matthew? Mark? Luke? (For Matthew's point of view see also §144 I.)

3. What did they hear, in each account? From whom, in each account?

4. Allowing for all the differences, how would you describe most generally, the nature of the experience that awaited the women at the tomb?

5. Again speaking most generally, what is the message? How does it relate, if at all, to any experiences that we ourselves may have had? What is its emotional content?

6. Who, according to these accounts, were the first "apostles" ("ones sent")? To whom were they sent?

SECTIONS 149-151 *Records*   (pages 189-191 *Parallels*)

Theme I: The Resurrection Experiences

Note: Here again the questions are along the line not of "Did this really happen?" but "What happened?"—to which might be added, "What is this appearance for? What is its purpose and meaning?"

1. For a first-hand account of such an experience see Acts 22:6-11 and First Corinthians 15:3-8.

2. What similarities, if any, between Paul's experience and that of the women at the tomb?

3. What difference, if any, did Paul find between the form in which Jesus appeared to others and to him?

103

Theme II: The Lukan account, §149 and §150

1. §149: Within what course of events, in what atmosphere, does this event take place? What is the state of mind of the disciples in A-D?

2. How do you account for the disciples' not recognizing Jesus?

3. "Slow of heart" (E): how? "To believe in": what? What way of understanding the scriptures is required here? Compare §150 D, "then opened he their minds."

4. When and under what circumstances did the two travelers recognize Jesus?

5. What are the lines of development of their experience and their insight?

6. §150: Within what course of events, in what atmosphere, does this experience take place?

7. "Terrified" (B): why?

8. "Supposed that they beheld a spirit" . . . "handle me and see": What point is at issue here? How does this difficulty with "a spirit" in first-century Hebrew thinking compare with our modern difficulty with a *bodily* resurrection? How has this difference come about?

9. "Thus it is written" (D): In what way are the disciples to understand the scriptures, and what are they to understand in them as a result of the experiences in §149 and §150?

10. In what way or ways is Jesus' "departure" in F different from his first departure in §139-146 (his arrest and execution)? What has happened to them between these two events?

11. What do these two stories in §149 and §150 offer us as indications of the way in which faith and experience develop? Of how a new and startling experience affects all previous experience? What do they tell us about our own ways of growth?

Theme III: The Matthew account, §151

1. Where does this event take place? Where do the events in the Lukan account take place?

2. What mission is given to the disciples in C? Compare §150 E Luke.

3. What promise is given to the disciples in C? Compare §150 E Luke.

THE QUESTIONS

The Fourth Gospel

John

Nothing gives a clearer indication of the difference between the Fourth Gospel and the other three than comparing the introductions to Luke and John. Luke's preface introduces a work that is clearly intended to be narrative: straightforward, businesslike, comprehensive. But the Prologue to John, what does it introduce? Words almost fail us, but we can try. What will this Gospel be *doing*? Surprising phrases come to mind. It will move within the areas of poetry, meditation, music. It will go out of this world; it will come into this world from the space beyond it or the depth within it.

John is like poetry in the way it presents its facts, reporting them briskly, clearly, vividly (no other Gospel tells a story so well) and then moves with energy and grace into exploring the feeling aroused by the story and the meaning it contains. The word "sign" as it appears in John hints at this process. A strongly negative word in the first three Gospels, "sign" in John carries the simple meaning of a sign by the roadside; it points to something beyond itself. These beautifully told stories are signs; and the reader who looks beyond them, following the author-poet's pointing finger, will come to the poetic and meditative truth of their meaning.

For instance, chapter 6 of John begins with a small story, complete with vivid detail and brisk conversation, about the multiplying of a few loaves of bread into an amount that will feed five thousand people. The story is a "sign," and we are invited to follow the pointing finger into a meditation on the true Bread of Life. Modern readers have trouble with the literary device that presents this meditation and others like it as spoken by Jesus himself. We take it all as flat fact (as if a tape-recorder had been there) and find the statements megalomaniac—forgetting that they are poetry, meditation, in which *meaning* is the goal and all kinds of literary techniques are put to work toward its development. A mental exercise might help: every time Jesus says "I am the life, the bread, the truth, or the way," we might think of the author as saying, "At this point I looked at him and said in my heart, 'You are the life, the bread, the truth, the way.'"

This exercise can free us from our literalism and help us move into the heart of John's meditation, in chapter 8. There the phrase I AM moves in a sweep of imagery all the way from the simple *ego eimi* ("it's me") of Greek idiom to the great I AM of Jahweh in the burning bush and presents this full range as Jesus' consciousness of himself. This is not a portrait of megalomania; it is a meditation on human nature and on the promise made in the Prologue that human beings can indeed, by looking at the full meaning of Jesus, receive "the right to become the children of God," and partake of his I AM, his being. And this in its turn is not megalomania; for though John more than all the other Gospels makes Jesus a mighty and commanding figure, John more than all the other Gospels stresses Jesus' derivativeness and dependence upon God. "The Son can do nothing of his own accord, but only what he sees his Father doing . . . I can do nothing on my own authority . . . I seek not my own will but the will of him who sent me" (John 5:19, 30 Revised Standard Version). If we partake of this I AM, we too will move in freedom and power within our dependence on God.

The Fourth Gospel is like music in the way it develops its themes. There is no use expecting its thought to move in straightforward, linear fashion like a piece of expository writing. That way lies confusion; but there is another way. We can get close to John's ways of statement by thinking of a quartet or a symphony. A theme is stated. It is dropped and another one is stated; then a third. Then theme A recurs, phrased a little differently in the light of what has happened in between. Then B and C may play a kind of duet. Then all three are gathered together in some kind of resolution, and theme D is introduced. And so on, until at the end everything is gathered together in a glorious summation and consummation.

This same musical process works upon the words that appear in the Prologue and again in the final prayer of Jesus in chapter 17. Word . . . light . . . life . . . world . . . truth . . . glory . . . Father . . . made known: in the beginning and at the end they are the same. But in between comes all the power of the music-of-idea, blending and developing the themes to a point where the words of the ending have acquired overtones and resonances that could only be guessed at in the words of the beginning.

John is the work of a writer whose central image and music come from an inner reality. "Whoever loves me will keep my word, and my Father will love him, and we will come to him and make our home with him" (John 14:23 Revised Standard Version adapted). This poet, this meditator, this musician, has loved Jesus, "kept his word," and freely given the risen Christ his only real home, the human heart. Speaking first as the resistant crowds of chapters 1-12 and then as the receptive disciple of chapters 13-17, he says to Jesus, as Jacob said to the angel, "I will not let you go unless you bless me."

And he has made the blessing that he received available to us. How can life, life itself, be transmitted by the printed page? It seems impossible; and yet it seems to happen as we read the Fourth Gospel. Its author is mediator for the Mediator. He speaks only the words that he has heard in his heart as spoken by the one who says, "The word which you hear is not mine but the Father's who sent me" (John 14:24, Revised Standard Version). And the words which we hear are spirit and life.

The foregoing may have alerted you to the fact that the Gospel of John requires of you a different style of leadership. You will have to be more directive, more in the driver's seat than you were when leading the Synoptics, as you and the group will have to work on the Johannine material in a very different way. But if you have managed to resist all temptations to do John before completing the Synoptics, you all will have had enough time together to learn one another's ways and acquire individual strengths; and the group will be able to tolerate some change in your style and accept your direction without being stifled by it.

The first part of your direction, beginning with the Prologue, will involve closer attention and a more searching imagination applied to individual large words. The word "believe," for instance, will need to be looked at for its meaning in context every time it appears if you and the group are to come to a full sense of its meaning in this Gospel. More than most writers, the author of John encourages words to mean what he wants them to mean—and that is many things, with overtones piled on overtones in a richness that defies any one definition of the word.

The second part of your direction will involve speed. While the Synoptics are an accumulation of short units, which can be looked at individually more or less at leisure, John comes in much larger units of a chapter or more, which must be looked at as a whole.

A typical unit is along these lines: a story; then a dialogue between Jesus and his hearers, shading off into a meditation by the author. The point is that the *whole thing* is the unit with which you and the group must work, holding each portion in your minds and letting its parts act and interact with your discussion.

To help this longer-unit approach maintain itself as you and the group work with John, I have set up questions in units. A unit may be done in one, two, or three sessions; it doesn't matter. The main thing is to hold yourself and the group to the concept of a unit of rich meaning waiting for you all to explore it as a whole.

If you ask at this point, "Who then can teach John?" you'll be right. But somehow it comes off. Once you have established that John cannot be approached like the Synoptics, perhaps the best way to "teach" this Gospel is simply to let it happen. Let it be an *experience* for the group, as poetry is for the attentive reader, as music is for the attentive hearer. Encourage them to be attentive, and then just let this Godspell happen to them.

Part I
The Book of Signs

John, Chapters 1-12. Eight Units. ─────────────

UNIT ONE   Prologue (cf. §1, Luke preface) *Records* §152; §153-154, John the Baptist §155-156, new followers.

UNIT TWO   *Records* §157. "Beginning of signs" §158-159. Meaning, §160-162.

UNIT THREE   *Records* §163-171. Baptism and the woman at the well.

UNIT FOUR   *Records* §172-177. The works of healing.

UNIT FIVE   *Records* §178-184. Feeding the multitudes and the bread of life.

UNIT SIX   *Records* §185-193. Jesus' origins. "Before Abraham was, I am."

UNIT SEVEN   *Records* §194-198. Seeing and blindness. Good and bad shepherds.

UNIT EIGHT   *Records* §199-208. Resurrection. Death and life, life and death.

The Fourth Gospel—Gospel of John. As with the Synoptics, references are keyed to H. B. Sharman's *Records of the Life of Jesus,* referred to as *Records.*

UNIT ONE

SECTION 152-156 *Records*

Theme I: Differences between the Fourth Gospel and the first three

1. Read Section 1, way back at the beginning, Luke's preface, asking one question: what kind of piece-of-writing would you expect the one that follows this preface to be?

2. Read §152, asking the same question.

3. Go through §152, taking note of the important and recurrent words ("life," "light," "word," etc.). How many of these are familiar from previous work with the Synoptics? The idea is to prepare the group for the fact that there will be many new words, many new concepts, and even familiar words which may have a different meaning (e.g. "believe" here and later at "sign"). Remind them of the work done previously on treating words as if they did not know the meaning, and establishing it gradually out of the text. Encourage them not to assume that they know what the word "believe" means; it is a very rich word in John and should not be restricted by our previous assumptions. Try to take it each time afresh and see what it means in that particular context.

Theme II: The Word

1. Now take the word "Word" and work out its emerging meaning through all its appearances in §152. What is said about the Word in verse 1? in verse 3? And so on. (Skip B and D for the moment.)

2. What do you make of the Word being referred to as "him" in verse 3?

3. What do you make of the identification with life and light?

4. "The Word became flesh . . . Jesus Christ . . . the only begotten Son": What is the process described here?

5. "Hath declared (the Father)": What do you make of this verb "declared" as applied to the activity of the Word?

(Needless to say, the group needs all possible translations to open up this stretch of material.)

Theme III: John the Baptist. New followers.

1. What was John the Baptist's relation to Jesus according to §152 BC, §153, and §154?

2. How does the dialogue develop in §155 and §156? (This question calls attention to the indirect, in-depth nature of the dialogue in this Gospel.)

UNIT TWO

SECTION 157, 160-162 *Records*
"Beginning of Signs": meaning

There's not a lot of material to cover in this unit. This will give you a leisurely time in which to pick up the material not covered (if there was any) in the first unit. Also, this material is properly part of the whole sweep of the baptism/living water theme of Unit Three. So it is good to think of this as primarily a bridge unit from One to Three.

General Theme: Baptism/living water; with water and with spirit. First pick up on §154 D for contrast of baptising with water and baptising with the Spirit.

Theme I: Water into wine, §157

1. Read the story and savor it. Encourage the group to experience it—to move into it, and its details.

2. "Sign," "glory," "believed on": What is the meaning of these phrases *in this context?* Contrast meaning of "sign" (proof—see §88) in first three Gospels, and here, where it seems to have a favorable meaning, more along the lines of the sign along the road that points the way to where you want to go. Here sign points to a meaning beyond itself. So:

3. What is the meaning that this story points to? In what way did Jesus "manifest his glory" by it?

Theme II: Cleansing, §159

1. What does the story of the cleansing of the Temple point to in the light of this whole theme of baptism/cleansing?

2. What is Jesus' interpretation of the whole idea of "temple" in EFG?

3. §160: Read and comment.

Theme III: Spirit, §161-162

1. Nicodemus story. Note dialogue, which proceeds in the same underground-stream way as dialogues in §155 and §156. Also

double-meaning words: "anew" can also mean "from above"; "spirit" (as in most languages) means both "breath" or "wind" and "spirit." So also in Genesis 1, the Hebrew word for "spirit" is also "wind." When these two meanings interact there are many overtones; encourage the group to work on and with them.

2. What points are made about "spirit" in the course of this dialogue?

3. What is the meaning of "believe" in §161 G verse 12?

4. Jesus seems to consider all that he is saying to Nicodemus an "earthly thing." What do you make of such an estimate? What does it say about our usual estimate of ideas, experiences, etc. connected with "spirit?"

5. Look back at and develop the meaning of Hebrew Bible story about Moses and the serpent (Numbers 21:4-9). How does it illuminate this reference to Son of man being lifted up? What is the meaning of "believe" in §162 A verse 15?

6. Point out that in John it is often impossible to tell when Jesus stops talking and the author begins making his own comments. The break in §161-162 is a good example. The group's guess is as good as anyone else's. What do they think? Do the quotation marks come at the end of §161? If not, where?

Theme IV: Judgment

1. Who does the judging, according to §162 B?

2. How does the judgment come about, according to §162 C?

118

UNIT THREE

SECTIONS 163-171 *Records*
Continuing the double theme of baptism and living water

Theme I: Relation of John the Baptist and Jesus, §163-167

1. What is John the Baptist's position concerning Jesus? Especially "this my joy"—"increase/decrease": why and how?

2. What different things are said about the "coming one" in §166? Related to what, if any, earlier material?

Theme II: The Samaritan woman §168-169

1. Background: Why did Jews have no dealings with Samaritans? How unusual was it for a properly-behaved Jewish man to speak to a woman in public? In view of this, how surprising is Jesus' behavior to this woman?

2. What is the course of the conversation here, between Jesus and the woman? How direct? How down-to-earth? What is its mood? What are its overtones? What are its implications?

3. What thread or threads of concepts, ideas, facts, is the conversation strung on?

4. What does this conversation contribute to the whole developing theme of water/living-water/baptism/water-into-wine?

5. What is the point at issue in the dialogue of E? "Salvation is of the Jews": What meaning, if any, does this phrase have for us today?

6. What effect does this conversation have upon the woman? (See also §170 B.)

Theme III: Jesus, the disciples, and the Samaritans, §170-171

1. What about the conversation in §169, if anything, would or could put Jesus into the state of mind described in §170 CDE?

2. How would you describe this state of mind?

3. What is the point of the harvest imagery in DE? What kind of comment does it make upon the events just preceding, in §169?

4. What is the reaction of the disciples to Jesus' conversation with the woman?

5. What is the reaction of the Samaritans of that city?

UNIT FOUR

SECTIONS 172-177 *Records*
The Works of Healing

Theme I: The "second sign"

1. Read §172. No special questions unless some arise.

2. §173: What happens in this story? If it is a "sign" (C), what does it point toward?

Theme II: Healing—"getting on one's feet," §174-175

1. What is the man's situation?

2. What is Jesus' part in this healing?

3. In what way or ways does this story enlarge upon and develop the story in §173? If it too is a sign, where is it pointing?

4. "Jews": What are we to do about this hardening of attitudes and stiffening of lines observable in this Gospel? What is the reason for it? What was the historical situation between Christians and Jews at the time when John was written (or, better phrase, in the days of the early church)? (Cf. Acts 4; 5:17-end; 12:1-5, for example.)

Theme III: Work

1. What is the "work" of the Father in §174-175 that Jesus observes?

2. What is the accusation of the "Jews" in §175 C verse 18?

3. Taken simply as a parable, how does the image in §176 A answer this accusation?

4. What is the work of the Father in §176 B?

5. What is the work of the son, according to §176 B-D?

6. What is the meaning of the word "judgment" in this section and §177 A? Compare §162 BC.

Theme IV: Witnesses

1. What are the credentials of "witnesses to" Jesus in §177?

2. What, in §177 F verse 44 makes "belief" impossible?

3. What is the meaning of the word "belief" in this section? (See verses 44, 46, 47.)

UNIT FIVE

SECTIONS 178-184 *Records*
The Bread of Life

Theme I: Bread, §178-181

1. §178: a "sign," which points in what direction(s)? (See also §179) (Get story clear and vivid, spend time on details; and note that the Greek word for "to give thanks" in §178 G is "eucharistein" in Greek.)

2. §179 A: What prophet is referred to here? What Hebrew Bible prophet produced food miraculously? (See I Kings 17:8-16.)

3. §181: What is the meaning of Jesus' comment in verse 26?

Theme II: Bread and manna

Work on § 182 ABC, compare § 176.

1. How is this theme developed in AB?

2. How is it tied in with manna in BC? With work? (Compare §176.)

Theme III: Jesus as the Bread of Life, §182

1. I AM, C verse 35 and F verse 41; cf. §180 C: and note that all three are the same Greek phrase, *ego eimi*, which has a wide range of meaning from just "it's me" to the "I AM" that we will meet soon; a good example of the stretchability of words and concepts in this Gospel.

2. In what senses can a person be "bread" to other people? F-I.

3. What connection, if any, does DE have with the bread theme which it interrupts?

4. J: Why is this idea so offensive to the "Jews?" (See Genesis 9:4.)

5. §183 A-C: Why is it so offensive to the disciples?

6. "The flesh profiteth nothing," §183 A: What does this passage have to say about earlier statements on eating and drinking the flesh and the blood?

7. What echoes, or overtones, or reverberations (some such word—maybe you can find a better one) do you find between this whole theme of the bread of life and the eucharistic bread? To what extent do you think such a connection is intentional on the part of the author?

UNIT SIX

SECTIONS 185-193 *Records*

Even if you do not do these two chapters in one session, point out to the group that they form a dramatic unity of tension, danger, division, discussion (even angry argument) leading up to the affirmation of § 193. Perhaps re-read § 162 B verses 17–21 as a prologue to it.

Theme I: Tension with Jesus' brothers over "my time," §185-186

What are the issues involved in this tension?

Theme II: Tension with "the Jews" over Jesus' authenticity, §187-189

1. §187: What is the point at issue in A?

2. How does Jesus answer it in B? What test of his authenticity does he set up in verse 17?

3. What is the point at issue in §188 AB? How does Jesus deal with it?

4. What is the point at issue in §189 A? How does Jesus deal with it? What happens?

5. "Ye shall seek me" (D): What is Jesus saying here about his origin and "where he is going?"

6. D: What do "the Jews" think he is saying?

7. E: "Spirit" in this is related to what? (Compare §169 CE.)

8. "Jesus was not yet glorified": meaning?

9. What is the point at issue in F? In G? What is Nicodemus' test of authenticity in H?

Theme III: The woman taken in adultery, §190

This material is more like Luke than John, and is supposed to be a stray from Luke. But deal with it here if group wants, and if you haven't done it at some Lukan point, for instance at the end of § 135. The best general questions are: What is the point at issue between Jesus and the religious folks? How does Jesus deal with it?

Theme IV: Back to Jesus' origin, authenticity, and nature

1. What is said about Jesus' origin and nature in §191? What echoes are there of earlier passages?

2. What is the line of argumentation and debate about origin in §192?

3. "Who art thou?": What answer to this question does Jesus give in §192?

4. "I am," verse 24 and 28: meaning of this? Comment on it as a buildup for what is to come, if nothing more. (Italics indicate no "he" in Greek.)

Theme V: Freedom and truth, §193

1. What is the point at issue between Jesus and his interlocutors in §193 A?

2. What freedom? What truth? How does truth make free?

3. What is the point at issue in B? What is Jesus saying about the origin of the kind of thinking his interlocutors are doing?

4. How does the argument continue in C? Note the frequent appearance of the word "word" throughout this section (Greek *logos* throughout). How tied in with truth is "the word" in this section?

Theme VI: "Before Abraham was, I am," §193 EF

It should be apparent by now that much two-level discussion is going on here, in the author's best style. Jesus is trying to lift the level of thought—if not of his hearers, at least that of ours. And this discussion reaches its climax in EF here.

1. What is the point at issue in E? What is Jesus' answer?

2. What is the continuation of the answer in F? What is the fullest possible meaning (*all* the way from minimum to maximum) of the affirmation "I AM." What Hebrew Bible echoes are there?

UNIT SEVEN

SECTIONS 194-198 *Records*

Theme I: Relation of sin to sickness, §194 AB

1. What is the disciples' assumption about this, in A?

2. What is Jesus' answer to the problem they raise, in A and B?

Theme II: Healing the blind man, §194-196 A

1. What are outstanding features of the healing, in C?

2. What are the outstanding feaures of what follows in D?

3. What are the points at issue in B and C, §195?

4. §195 D: On what does the blind man base his belief in Jesus? (Compare §194 D.) How extensive it it? What happens to it in §196 A?

5. What is the meaning of "belief" in this episode?

Theme III: Tension with opponents, §196 B-198

1. What is the point at issue in this continuing dialogue?

2. What is said about the opponents in §196 B? Who would you say that these opponents and questioners are, in modern terms?

3. To whom is §197 addressed? What is the point of the parable/image in A? Of the extension and slightly different development of the image in B? In CDE?

4. How is all this climaxed in §198?

5. What familiar themes are there in §198? What new ones?

UNIT EIGHT

SECTIONS 199-206 *Records*

Theme I: Life, death, belief, §200-201

1. Pick up all possible points in the story of Lazarus: imagery; characters; reactions of Jesus in the episode.

2. To what is this "sign"/story pointing?

3. Note many different uses, on many levels, of the word "believe," e.g. in dialogue with Martha in §201 B; with sisters in CDE.

4. When we look at and experience, so far as we are able, this whole story, its dialogue, its event, where are we in our understanding of, or feeling of, the meaning of the words "life," "death," or "belief" as John is using them here? ("Glory" comes later, though even it is mentioned in §200 A and §201 D).

Theme II: Death, §202-205

1. §202: Why death impinging, and from whom?

2. §203: Why death impinging, and from what?

3. §204: Death impinging, from what?

4. §205: Death impinging, from what?

Theme III: Jesus and his death, §206

1. BC: What does the image of the grain of wheat say about Jesus' attitude toward his own death? About death in general?

2. What is Jesus' attitude toward his death in D? In E and F?

Theme IV: Glory, §206

1. By what process is the Son of man to be glorified, according to B? According to D?

2. What is the point at issue in the dialogue in EF? What does it add, if anything, to the thought-development of this section's basic themes?

3. What does F add to this Gospel's development of the theme of light? (Compare § 162 C; § 152 A verse 4; § 191 A; § 200 B.)

SECTIONS 207, 208 *Records*

This is a general, poetic summary of Chapters 1–12, the Book of Signs, and as such you can find just about any theme you've looked at up to now, threaded on the general theme of belief versus unbelief. So one good thing to do might be to think back over the whole to review what these two words have come to mean in John through the many different settings in which they have been used. Reference points would be: § 182 AE; § 192 A–C; § 196 B; § 162 BC; § 187 B; § 177 A—I'm picking up here not just the "Belief" spots, but the material on light, on blindness, on judgment—all of which connects with John's understanding of the word "believe," to my mind.

Now you are ready for the Book of the Disciples.

Part II
The Book of the Disciples

John, Chapters 13-21. Nine Units. ─────────────

UNIT ONE   *Records* §209. The Footwashing.

UNIT TWO   *Records* §210. Absence/Presence.

UNIT THREE   *Records* §210 continued. The Comforter.

UNIT FOUR   *Records* §210 continued. The Commandment to love.

UNIT FIVE   *Records* §211. The vine image. Absence/presence again.

UNIT SIX   *Records* §212. Synthesis of themes. The great prayer.

UNIT SEVEN   *Records* §213-216. The two hearings.

UNIT EIGHT   *Records* §217-218. Last events.

UNIT NINE   *Records* §219-222. Appearances to the disciples.

General Introduction—Point out that we spent the earlier sessions on what is known in scholarly circles as the Book of Signs; I might call it the Book of the Outsiders, because for the most part it deals with Jesus' contacts with questioning or hostile people, or the very beginnings of discipleship on the part of these who were to become the Insiders. If you liked, you might take a few minutes (10 or 15) to look back at those contacts. To trace the growing acceptance on the disciples' part and growing antagonism on the part of "the Jews": § 155–156, disciples; § 161, Nicodemus; § 169, people of Samaria; § 175–176, "The Jews"; § 180–182, the multitude; § 187–193, "The Jews"; § 194–198; and so on.

Now with §209 we are moving into the time with the inner circle in the upper room (not so-called in John but you know what I mean).

UNIT ONE

SECTION 209 *Records*

Theme I: Footwashing, A-E

1. B: What if anything like this is there in the Synoptics? *(I'm reaching here for the teaching "I am among you as a servant," plus of course anything else that people think of. Note that often themes that are stories in the Synoptics are teachings in John, and as here, Synoptic teachings become/are stories in John.)*

2. "What I do ye know not now . . ." (C): What is the meaning of Jesus' action in BC? "Know ye what I have done to you?" (D): What is Jesus trying to get across to the disciples? What does Peter think is the meaning of Jesus' act? What is its bearing, if any, on what Jesus seems to be trying to get across?

3. What are the ideas developed in CDE?

Theme II: Judas, BF-K

1. What is the development of the conversation here?

2. What is the tone/atmosphere of this exchange?

Theme III: The Hour—Now—Departure, L-O

1. What echoes do you find in this passage? Compare §206 B; §189 D.

2. "Now is glorified" (L): how? why?

3. What is the meaning of "glory" in context of Jesus' life?

Theme IV: The Way, L-O

1. "Whither I go ye cannot come": why?

2. "But thou shalt follow afterwards": how? (Look on at §210 ABC.)

3. What does the "new commandment" have to do with all this? (See §209 N, §210 FHJ.) Why does Jesus call it new?

UNIT TWO

SECTION 210 *Records*

The themes throughout this whole discourse (§209 through §212) are so intermingled that you will have to keep backing up and going forward and coming back again, so resign yourself to it. For instance, last time you went on into §210 when you were dealing with §209; and now you are going back to §209 M.

Theme I: Absence, §209 MO; §210 ABCJ

1. What are possible meanings of "whither I go" in §209 MO?

2. "You cannot go": why not?

3. What reason is given for Jesus' absence in §210 A?

4. §210 BC: How are they to know the way?

Theme II: Presence, §210 AGHJ

1. What kind of coming/presence is described in §210 A? What kind in G?

2. What is the point at issue in H verse 22?

3. What kind of coming/presence is described in H? Where are the conditions under which it comes about?

4. What gift does Jesus give the disciples for the absent time in J? What do you think is meant by "peace" here?

UNIT THREE

SECTION 210 *Records* continued

Theme : The Comforter, §210 F I; §211 JMN

Compare § 189 E verse 39.

1. What gift does Jesus give the disciples for the absent time in §210 F?

2. As you look at Comforter passages, keep two things in mind:

   a) What is said about the Comforter? Work this through in detail, as you did with the word "word" in the Prologue.

   b) What do these passages add to the presence/absence theme?

3. What is the meaning of the word "Comforter?" Look at all possible other translations, and note that the Greek word is *parakletos*, "one who is called to someone's aid."

4. "Whom the world cannot receive" (§210 F): why not? "Abideth": why? how?

5. "Spirit of truth": why truth? Why not life, for instance, or love?

6. What is the function of the Holy Spirit in §210 I? in §211 J?

7. "It is expedient . . ." ("a good thing," Phillips; "to your advantage," (§211 M) Revised Standard Version): why?

8. What is the function of the Holy Spirit in §211 M verse 8-11? In §211 N?

UNIT FOUR

SECTION 210 *Records* continued

Theme I: The Way and the World

1. "I tell you beforehand" (§210 K—Compare §209 F, verse 19): why? What if anything does this have to do with the activity of the Holy Spirit?

2. "Prince of this world" (§210 K—Compare §206 E verse 31): Who is he? What, if any, connection is there with events described in §209 FH?

Theme II: Commandment, §210 H

1. Compare §209 N; §210 F verse 15; §210 H verse 21; §210 K verse 31. Are these the same commandment, or several different ones?

2. What do you make of a *commandment* to love?

3. Why does Jesus call it a *new* commandment?

UNIT FIVE

SECTION 211 *Records*

Themes continued from §210: absence and presence; the Comforter; the new commandment. Though they are not formally developed, they keep coming up, or being suggested and hinted at. So be alert for them as they seem to surface in the discussion, in whatever form, and be ready to look back with the group at other appearances of the same ideas in slightly different form.

Theme I: The vine image, A-C, D-H, K

1. "True vine": What does this phrase suggest, if anything, as to the meaning in this Gospel of the words "true," "truth," "truly" ("amen, amen")?

2. What is the full scope of the vine image? "Abiding"—cleansing—bearing fruit": What do these words add to the image?

3. How is the vine image connected with the disciples? With their mission, as described in E-H, K?

4. Keep in mind throughout this section, the twin themes of "abiding" and "pruning." Ask the group to hold as a continuing question how these themes tie the section together.

Theme II: Commandment, D-K Love (and hate)

1. What is the commandment(s) in DE? What does this portion add to what is said about commandment(s) in §210 H?

2. E: What is the difference between servants and friends?

3. What are all possible meanings of the phrase "lay down his life?"

4. "They hated me without a cause": do you agree? Why do "they" hate Jesus?

Theme III: Absence and presence, L-P, Q, S

1. Why do "these things" (K verse 1, and L) need to be said now? Why were they not said before?

137

2. Why is Jesus' absence "expedient" ("to your advantage") for the disciples?

3. "A little while" (O): What do you make of this dialogue with its repetition of bewilderment?

4. What does the image of birth-pangs in P have to say about the whole theme of absence and presence? About the theme of pain and fulfilment? About "a little while?"

5. Q: Ask what? When? Why? How does this compare with the "asking" theme in §85 D? What is said further about the theme of "asking" in §211 S?

Theme IV: Speaking in proverbs and/or plainly, R-end

1. In what way or ways would you say that Jesus has been speaking in proverbs/parables/images up to now?

2. In what way or ways would you say that he is speaking plainly now?

3. What do the disciples suddenly understand at this point? ("Now speakest thou plainly," T)

4. "Do ye now believe?" (U): What is the meaning of the word "believe" in this setting?

5. "I have overcome the world" (V): How so, in the light of all that we have read in John so far?

UNIT SIX

SECTION 212 *Records*

All the themes (or nearly all) that have been covered in the whole Gospel so far, here reappear and are woven together in a summing-up synthesis. It is worthwhile to spend a few minutes picking out the key words as we did earlier in § 152, The Prologue, noting how familiar they have become by now, and what our sense of their meaning is in this Gospel: glory; eternal life; name; truth; words; work; joy; world; love; one.

Theme I: The Words

1. How many of these words originally appeared in the Prologue, §152?

2. What meanings have they acquired for you since you met them there?

3. C: What work is described here? And for what purpose?

Theme II: The Prayer

1. What does Jesus ask for himself?

2. What does he ask for the disciples?

3. What does he ask for the world?

4. What is the connection among the three?

5. What is the relationship of Jesus to the Father? Of the disciples to Jesus? Of "those who believe" to the disciples?

6. "May be in us"; "may be one" (I); "perfected into one" (J): What kind of "one?" How is this one-ness achieved? Can we find any illustration of this theme of one-ness out of our own experience?

7. "Believe" (I); "know" (J): What is the significance, if any, of this change from "believe" to "know?"

8. What is the central aim of Jesus' work, according to J? According to K? According to L?

UNIT SEVEN

SECTIONS 213-216 *Records*
The two hearings

The story here makes an abrupt shift to narrative. Here it becomes appropriate to begin making comparisons to the accounts in the first three Gospels of the same events, Sections 139-145.

Theme I: The Garden. Jesus' Arrest. §213-214

1. Read §213 and ask for questions or comments.

2. §214: What does Jesus do in the garden before the soldiers come? (Compare with Synoptics, §140.)

3. What is Jesus' attitude toward events in B?

4. "I am he": what echoes are there of earlier material? (§193 F?)

5. "They went backward and fell to the ground": why? who?

6. Any comments on Peter's story, C and D?

Theme II: The First Hearing, §215

1. What are Jesus' responses to the questioning at this first hearing? How would you characterize his attitude?

2. How would you compare his attitude to that described in the Synoptics?

3. What features in the story of Peter as told here are not in the Synoptic account? Are there any differences in atmosphere?

Theme III: The Second Hearing, §216

1. What are Jesus' responses to the questioning at this second hearing? How would you characterize his attitude?

2. How would you compare his attitude to that described in the Synoptics?

3. How would you describe Pilate and his attitude here? What is his attitude toward Jesus? Toward Jesus' opponents ("the Jews")?

4. If, as we have thought, John deals with his material at several levels of meaning, the literal and what you might call the poetic, what are all the implications for you of such dialogue as that of C-F? N? Of Pilate's dialogue with the crowd, M-O?

UNIT EIGHT

SECTIONS 217-218 *Records*
Last events

Theme I: The Death of Jesus, §217

1. What are overtones of C verse 22 as a final comment on the dialogue between Pilate and the crowd in C?

2. What is the significance of "bearing the cross for himself"? Who carried the cross in the Synoptics?

3. What are Jesus' words from the cross in E-G? How do they compare with the words that are reported in (a) Matthew/Mark and (b) Luke in the Synoptics, §144?

4. What do these sayings suggest as to how Jesus met his death? (or "experienced the cross," if that's a better phrase; *all* phrases sound flat when dealing with this event; but at least they may serve to get the discussion going.)

5. How does the atmosphere of this event in John compare with that of the Synoptics in §144?

Theme II: The Burial Events, §218

1. How do the details of this event compare with the report of them in the Synoptics, §145 and §146?

2. What atmosphere is created by the differences? What effect does the John account have upon the reader? What is the significance of such details as those in BC? What are all their possible overtones, symbolic and religious?

UNIT NINE

SECTIONS 219-222 *Records*
Appearances to the disciples

(None of the following questions on Sections 219, 220, 222, do justice to the mysterious and poetical quality of these appearances—just as it is almost impossible to find non-pedestrian questions for § 149 and § 150 Luke. The best one can hope is that they will lead into a discussion that will bring out or suggest these qualities.)

Theme I: At the Tomb, §219

1. What is the significance of the details about the linen cloths (C)? "He saw and believed" (C verse 8): What is the meaning of "believed" here?

2. How does Mary Magdalene's experience develop in DE? How could she "suppose him to be the gardener?" Why didn't she recognize him? What is the meaning of verse 17?

Theme II: Jesus Appears, §220

1. What are the characteristics of the appearance in A-C? Of the appearance in E? Why the emphasis on wounds?

2. What happens during these appearances? What is their purpose? What effect do they have on the disciples? On us?

Theme III: First Ending, §221

1. Scholars generally note that here we have a clear first ending to this Gospel. According to it, what has been the purpose of this Gospel?

2. "Believe... believing": Is it the same meaning for the word in both places? What are all meanings of this word, as they have emerged for you out of the study of this Gospel? What is the connection between "believing" and "having life?"

Theme IV: The Risen Jesus, §222

1. What are the characteristics of the appearance in A? What is the

143

situation in which it takes place? How do the atmosphere and setting affect you?

2. Meaning of the dialogue in B? Note: the word translated as "love" here is actually two Greek words. The ones marked with a 3 are *agape*, "love as that of God or Christ to us, and our love to him and to our fellow creatures thus inspired" (so says my Greek dictionary). The ones marked with a 4 are *philia*, friendship.

3. What is the point of the different commissions given to Peter in B?

4. What is the meaning of the dialogue in C?

Theme V: The Second Ending, §223

1. Note that this is the second ending—cf. §221.

2. Who is the disciple mentioned in A? Have we had any clues throughout as to his identity? Is he ever directly named?

3. Which ending do you prefer: §221, or §223?

THE GROUP

Procedures

Membership

Who might be interested in taking a fresh look at the Gospels? Look for:

- Those who are suffering from overfamiliarity with the text, to the point where it has gone dead on them.

- Those who know little or nothing about the text—who may actually be reading it for the first time.

- Those who want a first-hand experience of the Gospels, not a study *about* them.

- Those who are dissatisfied with traditional Bible teaching as they have experienced it.

- Those who, for whatever reason, have come to feel the need of an inner center for their lives, and want to search Scripture for it.

This "fresh look at the Gospels" equalizes everybody. You will find that old and young, male and female, learned and unlearned, conventional and un-conventional people from all denominations, as well as those from other religious traditions or none at all, can all happily work together. All that is needed is openness of mind.

This type of Gospels study, however, is not for everyone. In it no one is ever *told* anything. No group conclusions are reached or aimed at. No final answers are given. There is no dispenser of knowledge; the leader's functions are solely to ask questions and keep the discussion moving. Not everyone wants to meet the Bible in this way, so in your publicity be sure to describe what it will be like, and even then expect some shrinkage in the early days. If the group is going well, word will get around and you will have some newcomers.

Most of you will be operating within the structure of some meeting, church, or synagogue. If so, it is of course important to get the permission, support and encouragement of whoever is in authority and to find space within the building for your meetings.

It is equally important, on the other hand, not to have such authority figures as members of your group, however interested and well-intentioned they may be. They are not personally responsible for the fact that their position of authority paralyzes the group; but almost invariably it does.

Leadership

Techniques of Leadership

As discussion leader your responsibilities are actually rather limited. You are there simply to see that all the important points, facts, and possible viewpoints about the text are brought out, so that each individual in the group may reach as full an understanding of the text as possible. You are there to ask questions, not to give answers. You are there to open possibilities, not to reach conclusions. You are there to encourage insights, not to give opinions. You are an *enabler.*

Some specific points of leadership:

1. Respect the time-limits you and the group have chosen. Start on time, and stop on the dot no matter how fascinating the discussion is at that point. If very rarely you need to take longer, get the group's consent, and make sure those who need to leave have the opportunity to do so.

2. Be sure that the members of the group know one another. Take time at the beginning for introductions, and if it does not seem too artificial, use name tags for a while. Keep using names of group members when referring to an individual's contribution to the discussion. It is assumed that you are not sitting in rows, but in a circle—preferably around a table, because of the books you will be using.

3. Do your homework; go over the text and the questions thoroughly yourself. Have a definite outline and procedure in mind and follow it, but not so rigidly as to lose a promising lead.

4. Be ready with questions to meet the developing interest of the group. This will come to be second nature after a while. Try to avoid questions that can be answered by Yes or No.

5. Hold the attention of the group to the material or theme directly under discussion, and move the discussion along. See that the thinking keeps progressing. Be alert for the moment when enough has been said for the time being. On the other hand, sometimes hold the group back when it wants to go over a theme too lightly.

6. Don't talk more than is absolutely necessary. The leader's job is to get others to talk.

7. Enlist as many members of the group in the discussion as possible, as soon as possible. Seldom, if ever, call on anyone, however, except in the most informal and tentative way.

8. Never be afraid of silence. The group needs time to think. At first ten seconds of silence will make you uneasy; later you will be able to tolerate much longer silent periods.

9. From time to time make summaries: indicate the ground covered, the trend of the discussion, the significant differences of opinion.

10. Encourage all possible points of view and insights into the text. Be sure that no one, however far out or conservative, feels neglected. Do not guide the discussion to a conclusion: the work should remain open-ended. *Trust the group.*

Problems in Leadership

Problems in leadership fall mainly into three categories: those connected with yourself; those connected with the text; and those connected with the group.

Yourself

1. *A feeling of inadequacy.* This is most overwhelming when you first start leading a group, but it will be with you off and on forever, so you might as well get used to it and begin right away learning how not to be overcome by it. If you find the group wanting you to know things that you don't know, just remind yourself that no law says you have to know everything. You only have to know how to ask the questions, find your way around in the text, and offer the absolute minimum of background information when it is absolutely necessary. If you feel cowed by the group getting out of hand or by some member of it trying to take over, remind yourself that you are the leader. Don't let anyone overawe you. Just keep plugging along.

2. *A feeling of adequacy.* This comes when you begin to feel in command of the material and at home with the method. You will find yourself overresponding to comments that you like, pushing for the answers you want, sharing plenteously from your newly-acquired great knowledge of text and background material, and generally taking over. This is almost impossible to avoid, human nature being what it is, and don't feel guilty about it. Just

resist temptation as much as you can, back away from your own power and *trust the group.*

The Text

It is easy to stray from direct relationship to the text, particularly in the early days of your leadership. Straying can come about in several ways:

1. You and the group can fall back into the prevailing modern habit of wanting to get all the facts, all the definite answers—wanting to have everything nailed down, in short. Before you know it you and the group will be studying *about* the text, not studying *it.* Commentaries will creep in and you will have lost your direct relationship to the text. Commentaries have their place, and can properly be used at home after the questions have been considered by the group. What usually happens, however, is that as the group learns how to work with the text and share insights, they will find the commentaries only saying what they have found out already. *Trust the text* and stay with it.

2. You and the group may find yourselves floundering around trying to find information that is not directly available in the text or conveniently available in anyone's knowledge—"pooling ignorance," someone has called it. This would seem to be a prime example of a need for dictionaries and commentaries, but actually what it indicates is that you have wandered off the main track, which is: "What does this text mean to us in this group now?"

3. Someone will think of something interesting; someone else will think of something interesting related to that; and before you know it you are off on a general discussion, having used the text as no more than a springboard to generalities. A good mental exercise here is to think of the text as the main trunk of a tree. You can allow the group to go out on one of the main branches for an insight that will illuminate the discussion; but if they begin climbing out on the smaller branches and even the twigs, you've lost it. After one trip out on a branch, come back to the main trunk, the text, and so keep the insights of the group text-centered and interacting with the text.

4. Individuals may begin quoting good things they've heard, or bringing in appropriate material that they want to read to the group. This can be another form of talking *about,* or it can be a genuine experience and reality to the person. The best way to handle it is to discourage direct quotation; say, "If you've read or heard something that is really full of meaning for you, say it in your own words." Then it will be a contribution to the discussion, not a final word on the subject. *Keep things open.* Trust the text and trust the group.

The Group

1. When you find yourself presented with a dumb, uncomprehending silence on the part of the group, ask where the trouble is, and re-formulate your question. If that fails, discard it and move on. Not every question you ask has to be answered. When you can't get any response to a question that you consider important, say "I'll leave this one with you to ponder on at home, and we'll move ahead for now." As you will find, the text nearly always gives you at least one more chance at any given subject or theme.

2. When you find—as you soon will—that some people in the group tend to talk a lot and others tend to be silent, take time at the beginning of the class to call the group's attention to this fact, in a general way—no specific mention of individuals—and say, "Maybe you fast talkers could count to ten, or more, before speaking up; and maybe you slow talkers could use that time to put in a word." This may produce some silences for a while, but just let them happen, and soon the slow talkers will be in the action, too. You may have to go through this process several times, at decent intervals; this situation tends to recur.

3. When you find one person talking too much, and so dominating the group, you can deal with it gently in public by saying things like, "What do others think?" or "Perhaps we should get back to the text now." But often you have to tackle the problem privately with the person concerned. Sometimes such a person will ask, "Am I talking too much?" To which a good answer is, "You don't talk too much, you talk too quickly. Try waiting until one or two others have spoken before you speak." If this person is someone who knows a lot and is eager to share the knowledge, point out that such input keeps the rest of the group from taking their own beginner's-mind approach to the text. To an opinionated person, point out that each person in the group needs to find his or her own approach to the material. In general, to a naturally talkative person you may even want to suggest a whole class session of silence in order to experience what can come out of silence and listening. It can be a revelation. To a troubled person with problems to share, you can suggest a practice of silence in the face of the text, listening to it and seeing what it says to her or his troubled situation, but not talking directly about that in the group. That silence too can be a revelation.

4. When you find that the group is irritated by one of its members to the point where they go into sullen silence every time he or she speaks, try to persuade such a person to keep a low profile for a month or two. The group will probably soon begin to be able to listen with open minds again.

151

5. When you find two members of the group getting into an argument, do not let the exchange turn into a continuing volley. Say, "What do others think?" If the arguers refuse to stop, say "Let's save this for you two to discuss together after class." And move on.

6. When you find, as you probably will sooner or later, that group members want to bring visitors, be welcoming but firm: visitors may come, but they must be silent, both for their own sakes and that of the group. If they talk, they will block the free flow of group discussion because they do not have the same background of shared work on the text; they will also effectively block themselves from seeing the kind of work that the group is doing. Similarly, if someone new wants to join the group, require silence for one class session, and if the person is interested in going on, offer a private briefing-session to bring her or him up to date on what has been done in the group so far.

To sum up: in general your attitude is that you will pay as much attention to individuals as you can, but that your main duty is to the group, and you are not going to let any individual dominate or disrupt it for any reason, however compelling.

Scheduling

Pace and Spacing of the Material

Your own sense of timing for the different kinds of material will come as you work with it. The following suggestions are intended only as a tentative guide for your first year of group leadership.

In general the idea is that a good look at all the Gospels material will take three years, from mid-September to mid-May each year—two years for the first three, or Synoptic, Gospels; and one for the Fourth Gospel, or John.

The Synoptic Gospels tend to fall handily into two parts: for the first year, Sections 17-74; for the second year, Sections 75-151. However, the framework is elastic. If you don't get past §70 the first year, §71-74 make a very fine introduction to the second year. In fact that §71-74 stretch of material is dual-purpose: it makes a fine conclusion for the first year's work and/or a fine introduction to year two. Leaders sometimes use them twice, for emphasis. It is probably the single most important stretch of material in the Gospels, and if I were to teach only one portion of them, it would be these four sections.

You will find that there is wide variation in the speed at which discussion of individual sections will move, and this is good, as it will keep the group from getting the habit of moving always at the same pace. Some sections deserve a good deal of time, others profit from being looked at more quickly.

As a sample of how the early sections might be paced, and how the tempo might vary, here is a rough outline of possible timing for Sections 17-54 in class sessions lasting an hour and a half.

1. Introductory talk, a look at §1, possible leaf through §1-16. One class session.

2. §1-16 leaf-through if not done. Discussion of text relations. §17, John the Baptist. One session.

3. §18 and §20, Baptism and Temptations. Two sessions.

4. §21-23, early ministry. One session.

5. §24-26, §28, early healings. One session.

6. §29 (go slowly here; an important section) and §30. One session.

7. §31-33, Jesus and his tradition. One session.

153

8. §34-35, and leaf-through of §36-38, general introduction to Sermon on the Mount/Plain. One session.

9. §36-38, the Lukan Sermon. Two or three sessions.

10. §36-38, the Matthew Sermon. Two or three sessions.

11. §39 (§40 briefly), §42, faith. One session.

12. §41, §43, §44, a miscellany. One session.

13. §45. An important session, on truth and hypocrisy. One session. Also §49, if possible.

14. §47-48, teaching in parables. Two sessions.

15. §50-54, more on faith. Two sessions.

You will find the material moving much more quickly between §55 and §70, leading into §71-74, which should move slowly, particularly §73 AB.

Possibilities in scheduling and using this material

Although the hoped-for development of your initial ten-week or shorter course would be the full three-year cycle of two years on the first three Gospels and a third year on the Fourth, many variations are possible. You will need to introduce and develop each of these short sessions within the framework of the specific group and situation in which it is to take place.

1. *A one-year program* focusing on significant episodes in the life of Jesus: baptism and temptations, sections 18 and 20; the healings, sections 24-29, 51-54, 75; meeting opposition, sections 30-33, 45, 130, 132; the end, sections 71-74, 124-126, 138-145; the resurrection, sections 146-151.

2. *Theme units.* Most of these take four or five weeks/meetings, and would make good introductions to the longer course.

> *"Who Am I?"* is one of the best, giving a central picture in only four sessions: Sections 18, 20, 71-74, 140.

> *The Sermon on the Mount.* Sections 36-38. About five sessions.

> *Faith.* Sections 39, 42, 50, 52 D-J, 75, 127. Four sessions.

> *The Parables.* Begin with sections 47-48 and the question, "Why teach in parables?" and pick up as many parables as you want: Sections 83, 92, 103, 105, 114, 118, 123, 129, 136. Two or more sessions.

> *Healings.* Sections 24-29, 33, 39-40, 51-54, 66, 70, 75, 98, 102, 111, 121. Three sessions.

154

Jesus and the Law.   Sections 32, 36 P-37 R, 115, 130, 132. Four or five sessions.

Jesus and Women.   Sections 42, 43, 46, 53 D-J, 64, 84. One or two sessions.

Kingdom of God.   Sections 21 C, 36 S, 38 D, 85 B, 112 A; parables of the kindgom, sections 47, 48; sections 103 D-H, 118, 123, 129 C-I, 136 E-S. Two or three sessions.

The possibilities are almost endless, and when you have familarized yourself with the material and the technique you will find favorite themes of your own and ways of organizing them.

3. Possibilities are endless also in the different ways this technique of group study can be used, and the Biblical material to which it can be adapted. Some of the tested ones are:

Enjoyment of Scripture I.   Most of Genesis and stories from the rest of the Pentateuch. A year's course.

Enjoyment of Scripture II.   Readings in Psalms, the Prophets, the Wisdom literature. A year's course or half year with:

Enjoyment of Scripture III.   Stories from the Hebrew Bible, told by members of the group and discussed in the group.

Events of Holy Week.   §137-145. Three or four sessions, very appropriate for the latter part of Lent.

The Birth Narratives.   §2-16. One session, appropriate for pre-Christmas.

Acts, Paul's Letters, selected.   A year-long course, focused not on the theology of it all, but on the experience of the early church.

Lectionary Study.   Most denominations, including Roman Catholic, now share a common lectionary—which means that in most churchs of the U.S. now, the same Bible readings are read each Sunday. Studying these selections each week before the Sunday when they are read makes a fine ecumenical project for a specific period, say Lent; and the practice may continue within specific congregations or groups.

Settings and groupings offer unlimited possibilities in all of this: high school settings, in colleges, at conferences, where a preliminary meeting with a central trained leader may prepare a group of leaders to deal with certain material in a much larger group, broken up into small units. All of this has been done successfully; there are undoubtedly many other possibilities.

Group Procedure

A page to be xeroxed and handed out to group members at the first meeting.

As a group we will read the text aloud from Henry Burton Sharman's *Records of the Life of Jesus.* Through discussion we will explore the text and our ideas and thoughts about it with no pressure to arrive at a specific conclusion or, in fact, any conclusion. All ideas and thoughts are welcomed for group thinking. We are together to enrich one another's thinking, not diminish it by argumentation and debate.

Guidelines for group members:

1. Maintain an attitude of *searching*—a "beginner's mind"—and try as far as possible to read as if for the first time.

2. Stay text-centered in comments and questions.

3. Talk briefly and to the point. Give others a chance to talk. Encourage those who hesitate to speak.

4. Listen to learn. Do not mentally shut off the ideas of another person by thinking of your own comments while that person speaks.

5. Contribute your ideas. Be honest and unashamed of possible lack of knowledge. Do your own thinking, independent of "authorities" (commentaries, for example).

6. Check your preconceptions and biases at the door. A helpful image is of a hatrack at the door on which you hang all your theological, academic, or other baggage; you can pick it up on the way out, but for the time of the class, leave it there.

7. Be sympathetic and ready to receive the opinion of another, rather than eager to correct or change it.

8. Honor silence if it develops. It may be a period for germination of new ideas, or a pause to reflect more deeply on what has been said.

9. Bring other translations of the Bible to the class and keep them open at the passage being studied. Often a different translation will shed light on obscure passages or add a deeper understanding of the text. Do not hesitate to refer to another translation in discussion. In speaking of what Christians commonly call the Old Testament, refer to it as "Scripture" or "The Hebrew Bible" as this is less offensive to non-Christian hearers.

10. If you come late to class, or have missed the previous meeting, be silent long enough to be sure that what you have to say will fit into the discussion and the spirit of the group.

Helpful Books

Two additional books of questions and suggestions for leaders:

1. *Transforming Bible Study*, by Walter Wink. Abingdon 1980. Especially valuable for its insight-deepening exercises, this books stems from the Jungian-centered Gospels study at Four Springs, California.

2. *A New Dimension in Old Testament Study*, by Sadie Gregory. Guild for Psychological Studies, 1980. Also coming out of the work at Four Springs, this small book asks stimulating inwardly-directed questions about Genesis, the Psalms, the major prophets.

A suggested reference library for Gospels study

1. *The New Oxford Annotated Bible with the Apocrypha.* Expanded Edition, Revised Standard Version; an Ecumenical Study Bible, Oxford University Press, New York, 1977. Sometimes called the Common Bible because of its wide acceptance, this is probably the most useful Bible for group and individual study.

2. *Good News Bible: The Bible in Today's English Version.* American Bible Society, New York, 1976. A readable and down-to-earth new translation with notes and line drawings that add greatly to its effectiveness. A valuable supplement to #1.

3. *Tanakh: A new translation of the Holy Scriptures according to the traditional Hebrew text.* The Jewish Publication Society, Philadelphia, 1985. Another valuable supplement to #1, offering a non-Christian perspective that is broadening and helpful.

4. *Understanding the Old Testament*, by Bernard W. Anderson. Prentice-Hall, 1975. Almost everything you need to know from a Christian point of view about the Hebrew Bible.

5. *The Enjoyment of Scripture*, by Samuel Sandmel. Oxford, 1972. The Hebrew Bible as seen by a Hebrew scholar. An excellent and stimulating book.

6. *Good News for Everyone: How to use the Good News Bible*, by Eugene A. Nida. Word Books, Waco, Texas, 1977. An insight into the many problems involved in translating the Bible fully and freshly into modern English.

7. *Can We Trust the New Testament?* by John A. T. Robinson. Eerdmans, 1977. A description for the general reader of what this past century of New Testament critical study has accomplished, and where we are now in enabling the text to speak openly and directly to us.

8. *Jesus of Nazareth*, by Gunther Bornkamm. Harper and Row, 1975. A fine example of the kind of scholarship described in Robinson's book above.

9. *Speaking in Parables: A Study in Metaphor and Theology,* by Sallie McFague. Fortress Press, Philadelphia, 1975. A stimulating and refreshing book that opens the parables of Jesus and the metaphor of his life to the possibility of new and evergrowing insight.

10. A good Bible dictionary. The ones put out by Harper and Row and by Westminster will give you background information on any Biblical subject in readily accessible, alphabetically arranged form.

11. A concordance geared to whatever version of the Bible you use most often.

12. *The Cotton Patch Version of Matthew and John* by Clarence Jordon. Association Press, 1970. "A modern translation with a Southern accent" that's great for breaking through piety. There are also Jordan *Cotton Patch Versions* of Luke, Acts, and Paul's Epistles.